SPOOKY

Michigan

*Tales of Hauntings, Strange Happenings,
and Other Local Lore*

RETOLD BY S. E. SCHLOSSER

ILLUSTRATED BY PAUL G. HOFFMAN

Globe
Pequot

An imprint of Rowman & Littlefield
Distributed by NATIONAL BOOK NETWORK

Text copyright © 2017 by S. E. Schlosser
Illustrations copyright © 2017 by Paul G. Hoffman

Map by Lisa Reneson © Rowman & Littlefield
Map border by Paul G. Hoffman

British Library Cataloguing in Publication Information available

Library of Congress Cataloging-in-Publication Data available

ISBN 978-1-4930-2713-2 (paperback)
ISBN 978-1-4930-2799-6 (e-book)

∞™ The paper used in this publication meets the minimum requirements of American National Standard for Information Sciences—Permanence of Paper for Printed Library Materials, ANSI/NISO Z39.48-1992.

Printed in the United States of America

For my family: David, Dena, Tim, Arlene, Hannah, Emma, Nathan, Benjamin, Deb, Gabe, Clare, Jack, Karen, and Davey.

For Ezra John and Mary Elizabeth Schlosser, my great-grandparents, who loaded their wagon with worldly goods and children and went north to live and work in Michigan.

For Loyd Victor Schlosser, my grandfather, whose stories of his early days in Michigan have taught me a great deal about laughter and courage and life. And for his siblings, Vernell, Ted, Ethel, Vera, and Wilma, who all lived in and loved Michigan.

* * *

Contents

Contents

Contents

1. Alger
2. Ann Arbor
3. Midland
4. Detroit
5. St. Martin's Island
6. Grand Rapids
7. Sault Sainte Marie
8. Grand Haven
9. Marquette
10. Tahquamenon Falls State Park
11. Saginaw
12. Monroe County
13. Marquette County
14. Wayne County
15. Grand Rapids
16. Central Michigan
17. Ann Arbor
18. Isle Royale National Park
19. Cheboygan
20. Detroit
21. Port Huron
22. Lansing
23. Detroit
24. Traverse City
25. Mackinac Island
26. Deer Park
27. Upper Peninsula
28. Grosse Pointe Woods
29. L'Anse
30. Kalamazoo
31. Detroit
32. Jackson
33. Detroit
34. Detroit

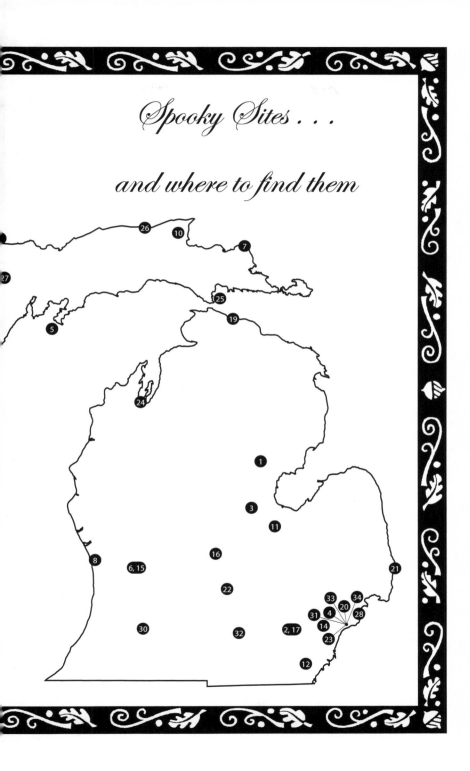

Spooky Sites . . .

and where to find them

Introduction

When my grandfather Loyd was nine years old, his parents packed their belongings and their six children into a wagon and moved from Ohio to Michigan, where they bought land to farm. For a year or two, they lived in Hillsdale County in the southernmost part of Michigan, but then Ezra John, my great-grandfather, heard of some farming opportunities in the town of Temple, Clare County, near the top of the state. So the family packed their wagons again and traveled north.

Listening to family stories of that period, I am strongly reminded of the wild frontier, even though the move to Michigan happened after 1910. Ezra John built a two-room tar paper shack for the family to live in. The parents slept in the big back room. The front room held the cooking stove and table. During the day, it was the family gathering place. At night, it was separated by a blanket on a rope. The three older boys—Loyd, Vernell, and Ted—shared a double bed on one side, and the three younger girls—Ethel, Vera, and Wilma—shared a double bed on the other. The iron bathtub was filled with hot water once a week during the winter so the children could take baths.

As a boy, Loyd chopped wood for the stove, carried water from the well, took care of the horse, and attended a one-room schoolhouse. Once the school bully threw my grandfather into a pit, so Loyd and his younger brothers ganged up on the bully after school and "took care" of him. The bully never bothered any of them again.

Grandpa described his family as "dirt-poor" farmers. One winter when Loyd wore out his rubbers, his father walked 9 miles into the town of Harrison to pick up a used pair of shoes that a family was giving away. The shoes were a worn-out pair of Oxfords that had holes in the toes and sole. Loyd's father carefully repaired the shoes with cardboard and burlap to keep the snow away from his eldest son's feet.

Sometimes the Schlosser family harvest was only forty bushels of potatoes that they put into a dug-out cellar. One winter they ate beans every day in order to survive until spring. They took family "outings" to pick huckleberries and blackberries for canning, typically gathering enough berries to can forty or fifty quarts for the winter. On one memorable berry-picking trip, a bear spooked the horses, and my aunt Ethel was thrown over the side of the wagon, where she clung for dear life to the sideboard until the horses were slowed and her brothers could drag her back inside.

Another time my grandfather was riding out alone to the berry patch when a bear spooked his horse. The horse threw him and bolted. Loyd was knocked unconscious by a stone and awoke to the darkness of night. He very cautiously walked several miles home, dizzy from a concussion and frightened by the possibility of encountering the bear again.

When the farm in Temple finally failed, Ezra John packed everyone up and went south to Midland, where he got a job at Dow Chemical. Loyd and his brothers finished high school in their new town. Then Loyd and Vernell bought a Ford Touring car, taught themselves to drive, and headed south to electrical engineering school in Washington, D.C.

As a child, I was frequently entertained by these and other stories of my grandfather's early days. I remember my excitement on my first trip to Michigan. I sat through the long drive, picturing one-room schoolhouses, hardworking farmers driving horse-drawn wagons, bears, and berry picking. To my surprise, I found a high-tech world with televisions, radios, large schools, and kids who dressed exactly like I did. I was shocked. Where were the horses and huckleberry patches? Alas, time had moved on for Michigan just as it had for my grandfather, and the state I visited was as modern as any in my home state of New Jersey.

If, as a child, I was a bit disappointed to discover a modern Michigan, I was delighted to find that her folklore reached back many thousands of years. From myths and legends recited around the fire to stories and tall tales from groups as disparate as French-Canadians, trappers, lumberjacks, lake captains, and railroaders, Michigan folklore is as colorful and varied as my grandfather's stories.

Tales like *The Talking Head* and *Nishishin Raises the Dead* reveal a world inhabited by native tribes living and loving and working together long before white men set foot on this soil. Other stories, like *A Father's Revenge* and *One Last Head*, show what happened when these two worlds collided.

The importance of the railroad industry comes to life in ghost stories like *The Engineer's Message* and *Ghost Train*. The world of the logger is highlighted in *The Wraith of the Creek*. And no Michigan collection would be complete without mention of the master lumberjack Paul Bunyan (*Paul Bunyan and the Witch*).

I believe the tales from Michigan that have moved me the most are those centering around the Great Lakes. Michigan is bordered by four of these five behemoth bodies of water, and much of her history involves ships and fishing. Superstitions, tragedies, dramatic rescues, and legends abound. One of my favorite stories is that of a seagull who warns a fisherman that his wife has been injured (*The Seagull*). Another tells the tale of a shipwrecked sailor who is rescued . . . by a ghost ship (*The Merchant*). And of course, the story of *The Wizard's Rope* warns sailors not to board a ship captained by a Master of the Winds . . . unless his wife remains at home.

Michigan is a state that has captured my imagination since childhood. I hope that this collection of stories encourages readers to take delight in the glorious color, variety, and history of the Great Lakes State, just as I do.

— Sandy Schlosser

PART ONE
Ghost Stories

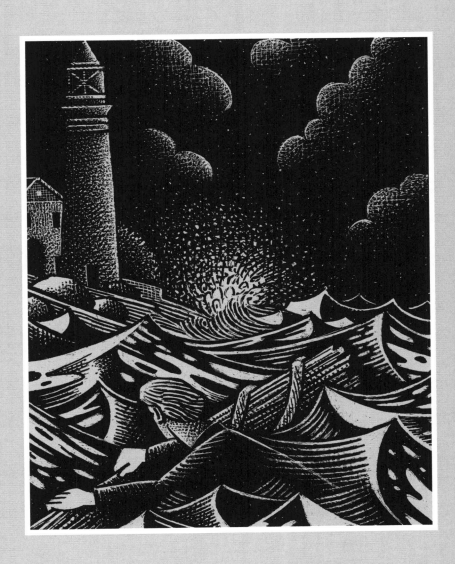

1

The Wraith of the Creek

ALGER

He left his tribe to work with the white lumbermen in Alger, changing his name to William Cloud. He even dressed in white man's attire and attended the local church on Sunday. It was a new life for him, and he was grateful when the lumbermen accepted him with little regard for his color or his birth. The lumberjacks started calling him "Cloudy," and they occasionally asked him to tell them some of the traditional stories from his tribe when they gathered around the fire at night.

The story they liked best was about the wraith that lived in the creek that powered the local log chute. The wraith was an evil creature that desired nothing more than to wrap its long arms around humans or animals and pull them down into the water to drown. At dusk, the wraith would slip out of the creek and hunt along its banks. Anyone passing near the creek from dusk until midnight should walk wary indeed, Cloudy told them, for the claws of the wraith could tear a grown man to bits in a few sharp blows.

The lumbermen liked to tease Cloudy about the wraith. Whenever he worked down on the log chute, some jokester would leap out at him from behind a tree, hands extended like claws, and grab him. Cloudy took the teasing in the good-natured spirit that it was intended, but he made a point of never going near the chute after dark. His uncle had been taken by the wraith when Cloudy was a small boy, and he would never forget the sight of his uncle's mangled body when his father and the other tribesmen pulled it from the creek.

It rained heavy and long that spring, and the creek was flooded almost to capacity. A large raft of logs was floated down to the chute, but the foreman decided to hold them back with a gate until the creek rose high enough to send them through in a mass. The order to lower the gate came through about 9:00 p.m. one stormy night in early April. Thunder was booming constantly, such that the lumbermen waiting in the cabin could hardly hear each other speak. Jagged lightning blazed across the sky, and the rain fell in heavy, chilly sheets. The thought of going outside in the storm did not appeal to anyone. Finally, the men drew straws, and Cloudy came up with the short one.

"Bad luck, ol' chap," said Ethan, a British man who was new to the lumber camp. "Watch out for that wraith of yours. It hunts the banks of the stream at this time of night, and this is just the sort of weather it likes best."

Cloudy glanced briefly at his comrade and nodded wordlessly. He clapped on his cap and slipped out the door before anyone else could speak. He knew that the Englishman meant no harm, but it was dangerous to speak of the wraith before going to the creek. Such careless speech might draw the attention of the very creature he hoped to avoid.

Cloudy was instantly soaked by the heavy rain and cut to the bone by the chilly wind. He hugged his coat tightly around him as he made his way silently through the pitch-black night toward the log chute and the waiting raft. It would take only a moment to lower the gate, and then he would run as fast as he could back to the safety of the cabin. He comforted himself with this thought as he approached the creek bank. He could hear the roar of the flooded stream long before he saw it, and within moments he was at the gate and tugging at the iron pins that held it above the water.

As he released the first pin, he heard a foul hissing sound from beside the floating raft of logs. Cloudy turned his head and saw a grotesque form rising from the swirling stream. It had a cat-like face, glowing yellow eyes, and long teeth. Its face was framed by wild, weed-strewn hair. Sharp spikes protruded from its spine, and dark slimy scales covered its lithesome body.

Cloudy gave a loud shout, hoping to scare the creature away. He tugged at the final pin, but it got stuck halfway out. Suddenly, the creature lunged out of the water. Cloudy leapt back, abandoning the recalcitrant pin to flee back up the path toward the distant cabin and safety. Behind him, the wraith howled once: a long, threatening shriek. Cloudy increased his speed, running blindly in the darkness as tree branches slapped at him and roots tripped his feet.

From behind him, he heard the sound of claws raking the muddy path as the wraith pursued him. The creature howled again, a sound that froze his blood even as it made his heart thump so hard that it hurt his chest. He heard the creature veer off the path suddenly, and then the sounds of pursuit ceased. Cloudy gasped and pushed himself harder, more frightened by the sudden silence than he had been when he saw the creature first rise from the waters.

THE WRAITH OF THE CREEK

Then the wraith dropped down from the branches of a tree right in front of him, blocking his way. Its yellow eyes glowed, and moonlight glinted against its slimy skin. Cloudy saw its long, thin arms stretch out toward him through the raging storm, claws extended. He gave one loud shout of despair, thrashing at the monster with his hands and feet. His cry was cut off suddenly by the lightning-fast movement of a razor-sharp claw, and the woods were suddenly still again, save for the sound of the chilly April rain.

Back in the cabin, the lumbermen waited with increasing unease for Cloudy to return. At first, they joked about the wraith. One man wondered aloud if Cloudy was hiding somewhere until after midnight, when the creature was said to return to its underwater den to sleep. But as the minutes ticked by, the men grew somber. Finally, Ethan volunteered to go down to the log chute and look for his friend. Several other loggers decided to accompany him. Though no one said anything aloud about the wraith, the men all loaded their guns before stepping out into the rainy night.

Within ten minutes, the men were standing next to the lowered gate, watching the water rushing down the chute. There was no sign of Cloudy, but after a moment, Ethan realized that the gate had not settled fully into the water. The men lowered the lantern to the level of the rushing water and peered into the depths at a large object partially obstructing the gate. It moved slightly in the current, and Ethan gave a sudden sharp cry as it flipped over, revealing the mangled face of Cloudy.

The loggers lifted the gate slightly and drew Cloudy up with pike poles. His body had been sliced to ribbons, and his head was almost completely severed. They could see teeth marks on his face, and parts of his arms and legs had been ripped away completely. Ethan picked up his friend's body while the other men stood in a ring around him, guns pointing in every direction. Keeping a sharp lookout for any sign of the creature that had killed Cloudy, the loggers hurried back to the safety of the cabin.

The next day, Cloudy's body was buried in a small clearing in the woods, far away from where the feared wraith lurked. The foreman instructed everyone working at the creek to keep their guns with them at all times, and no one was to go near the log chute after dark unaccompanied. News of the murderous wraith in the creek quickly spread through the lumber camp and the nearby village. Many of the loggers quit their jobs rather than risk their lives.

One night, a week after Cloudy's death, Ethan was awakened by a strange blue light hovering above his bed. He opened his eyes and found himself gazing into the shining face of William Cloud. The spirit warned Ethan to leave the lumber camp at once. The wraith had marked Ethan for its next victim the night he came down to the stream to look for his friend. If the Englishman stayed at the camp, he would share the same fate as Cloudy. Terrified, Ethan promised the apparition that he would depart at sunrise. Cloudy's ghost nodded gravely and disappeared, leaving the Englishman trembling in the darkness.

At daybreak, Ethan packed his belongings and left the camp. On his way out, he confided his story to the men who had helped him retrieve Cloudy's body. Soon word of Cloudy's warning spread throughout the camp, and by sundown, it was completely deserted.

With no one left to maintain it, the log chute fell into disrepair and slowly crumbled away, never to be replaced. In the depths of the stream, the wraith still lurks, watching for another victim. But it waits in vain, for the ghost of Cloudy appears to anyone foolish enough to wander near the stream, warning them away with terrible groans and piercing screams.

2

The Engineer's Message

ANN ARBOR

It should have been obvious right from the start that Johnny was going to work for the railroad. Even as a child, all his energy was concentrated on trains. In the cradle, he didn't want to hold my fingers, even though I was his own mother. He only wanted the wooden boxcars and engine that his Pa carved for him. As a toddler, his favorite game was "choo-choo train," and by the time he turned five, Johnny knew every engine on the local line.

Johnny's vocabulary bloomed with all sorts of colorful phrases during his school years. He spent every free moment at the depot and came home with stories about railroad engineers who were always taking chances by "highballing" (making a fast run) in an attempt to bring their train in "on the cat hop" (on time); about firemen who "batted the stack off of her" (worked an engine at full stroke); about incompetents who "danced on the carpet" (were called to an official's office to be disciplined) or appeared in "kangaroo court" (an official hearing or investigation that was held wherever most convenient). I think Johnny took secret delight in confusing me. His brown eyes would dance with laughter whenever he started using railroad lingo.

Still, when Johnny told me that his ambition was to become a "hoghead," I was taken aback. Mistaking my alarm for confusion, he laughed and told me that a "hoghead" was an engineer. Recovering slightly, I chuckled weakly, trying not to remember that my grandfather, a railroad brakeman, had slipped between the cars of his own train one day and had been crushed under its spinning wheels.

I vividly remembered the night we learned of my grandfather's death. I was awakened suddenly by the sound of my mother sobbing and my grandmother repeating something over and over again in tones of deep shock and denial. The sounds came from the kitchen, and I knew something bad had happened before I set one foot on the back staircase.

I shivered at the memory, and Johnny slipped an arm around me. "What's the matter, Ma? Did a goose walk over your grave?"

"Just a chill in the air," I said lightly. I didn't want to dwell on the memory, lest it bring bad luck to my boy.

Johnny got his first job as a cub operator on the Michigan Central Railroad straight out of school, and right from the start, he excelled. He was happy to be working on the steam trains; I could see it in his face every time he came home to visit.

A few months later, Johnny took a more active role as a brakeman on the line. With his long-range goal of becoming an engineer in mind, he then transferred to another line as a fireman. I knew it would not be long before he realized his dream. And within a few years, Johnny was indeed promoted to

THE ENGINEER'S MESSAGE

the position of engineer. The day he received his commission, he proposed to his pretty girl—a member of our next-door neighbor's brood whom he had known since birth. Katie and Johnny were married a few months later.

It wasn't long after Johnny became an engineer that I began to hear the stories. He was a "glory hunter," a reckless, fast-running engineer. Because Johnny wasn't afraid to take risks, he made several record runs during his career and soon was famous in railroading circles. He also became the father of two beautiful little girls, which made us very proud. He and Katie built a little house right next door to ours, and we looked after her and the girls whenever Johnny was away.

One night late in January, I awoke from a deep sleep, certain that I had heard Johnny's voice.

"Mama," I heard Johnny say again.

I turned over and blinked in the dim light coming from the streetlamp outside our window. Johnny was standing beside the bed, dressed in his engineer's uniform. He was gazing down on me tenderly. I sat up immediately.

"Johnny," I gasped.

He smiled and sat down beside me, as he had often done when he was little. He took my hand and said, "I want you to know how much I appreciate you and Pa. It couldn't have been easy, raising a headstrong boy like me, but you did a wonderful job."

Johnny's words filled me with a strange mixture of joy and fear.

"Aw, Ma, we both knew I was never going to 'get the rocking chair.' Not a glory hunter like me. No, I'm going to be working the 'Indian Valley Line' from now on."

In the dim light, I could see his beautiful brown eyes dancing as he casually threw his railroad lingo at me. I'd learned a lot of it since the early days when my little boy would tease me in the kitchen after school. To "get the rocking chair" meant to retire on a pension. And the "Indian Valley Line" was an imaginary railroad at the end of the rainbow, on which you could always find a good job and ideal working conditions. It was the place engineers went when they died.

Tears sprang to my eyes, and Johnny gently wiped one away with his finger. "I came to tell you that I'm alright. Take care of my girls for me."

"We will," I managed to say through my choked-up throat.

"I love you, Ma. We'll be together again real soon," Johnny said. He leaned forward, kissed me on the cheek, and then he was gone.

I fell back against my pillows, too stunned even to weep. My husband, who was a heavy sleeper, woke when he felt the thump. He rolled over and mumbled, "Are you alright?"

"Something has happened to Johnny," I said. "I think he's dead."

My husband jerked awake. "What?" he exclaimed.

I started sobbing then, and I told him about Johnny's visit. We held each other close for the rest of that long night, waiting for dawn and the news that would surely come with it. Just after breakfast, a representative from the railroad came knocking on our door. Johnny's train had fallen into a river when the bridge it was crossing collapsed during a snowstorm. Everyone onboard had been killed.

The days following the official notification of Johnny's death were mind-numbing. I clung to the words my boy had spoken to me in the moments after he died. Johnny had said he was alright, and I believed him. My son's body was gone, but his essence, his soul, everything that made him my Johnny was safe and well. And we would be together again real soon.

3

Followed Me Home

After Fred died, I sold the big house and moved into a charming little cottage in a nice neighborhood. Almost as soon as the moving van had left and my son had kissed me goodbye, my new next-door neighbor dropped by. She was also a widow, just a year older than me, and she liked genealogy and playing bridge almost as much as I did. It was the beginning of a lovely friendship.

I quickly discovered that Shirley had a quirky sense of humor and a deft way with words. Her tales about her family left me in stitches. My favorite stories were about ninety-year-old Uncle Charlie, who chased pretty girls down the hall of his nursing home and pinched the old ladies in the you-know-where when they weren't looking. There wasn't a week that went by when Shirley didn't have another tale to tell about Uncle Charlie.

I was eager to meet the old chap, even if it meant a pinch on the bum, but he died in his sleep before we could arrange it. I went with Shirley to his funeral—a closed casket, by Uncle Charlie's request—so I didn't even get to see what he looked like. They buried him beside his long-dead wife, who I understood from Shirley had nagged Charlie every single day of their married life.

15

Shirley and I tossed two bouquets of flowers down on Charlie's casket and wished him a good time in the next world. It was a sad day, but we figured Charlie would be happy chasing the pretty angels around heaven and getting into one scrape after another.

I attended the small funeral brunch at Shirley's house and then went home. The evening proceeded normally; at least, until I heard that funny squeaking sound the front door makes when it opens. I was puzzled. I knew I had shut the door firmly when I came in, and I was pretty sure I'd locked it too. I went in the hallway to investigate and found the front door wide open, as if someone had just walked in.

Behind me, Misty, my gray cat, started to purr. She walked delicately toward the front door and started twining herself around and around, as if she were rubbing against someone's legs in greeting. But there was no one there. My arms broke out in goose bumps. I hastily shooed Misty away and closed the door. The cat continued to purr and leisurely walked into the living room, as if she were dogging the footsteps of some invisible presence.

In the living room, Thomas, my ancient fox terrier, huffed a greeting to a very-empty-looking spot in the middle of the room and then settled back down in his basket to snooze. I hurried away to the kitchen to do something normal—like the supper dishes—and then went right to bed, telling myself I was being overly imaginative and silly.

The next morning, I found a few of the kitchen cabinets standing open, as if someone had been searching through them, looking for something to eat. Pretending that I must have left them open last night (I hadn't), I quickly closed them. I ignored Misty's purred greeting to someone who just happened to be occupying the empty chair across from mine as I sat at the table to eat my cold cereal. I pretended not to see the unfolded newspaper on the kitchen counter where I had definitely not put it, and I absolutely did not see one of the pages turn all by itself as I grabbed my keys and walked out the back door.

For almost two weeks, I ignored the invisible person living in the house with me, although he—it felt like a he—drove me crazy. He left cabinets open, scuffed up the rugs, rearranged the furniture to suit his fancies, and forgot to turn off lights. But when he started whistling off-key, I decided I'd had enough.

I'd told Shirley about my unwanted guest. She'd been reluctant to believe me until she came over one morning and found someone invisibly reading the newspaper. After that, Shirley gave me the name of a psychic whom she'd heard about, and I finally gave the woman a call.

Shirley wanted to be here when the psychic arrived, but she was called over to her daughter's house to babysit, and so she missed out on the grand entrance. The psychic was a nice, normal-looking brunette who stiffened as soon as she entered the house.

"Yes, you do have a ghost," she said, before I'd even had a chance to take her coat.

We sat down in the living room, and the psychic quickly made contact with the spirit. And what do you know? It was Uncle Charlie. Apparently, he'd seen me at the funeral and decided I reminded him of his first love, a woman named Linda. So he'd followed me home.

"I'm flattered," I said carefully, "but it isn't seemly for a widow to be sharing her home with a handsome bachelor such as yourself."

FOLLOWED ME HOME

As the psychic relayed my message to the ghost, I heard Shirley's car pulling into her driveway. I knew she would be over any minute. I wondered what she would say when I told her that Uncle Charlie had followed me home from the funeral.

"Charles has agreed to leave the house," the psychic said. I wanted to ask where his spirit usually resided, but I decided that was a personal question best left unasked. Then I felt a distinct pinch on my bum. I jumped and uttered a little shriek. A moment later, a feeling of emptiness filled the room.

"Charles is gone," the psychic told me, giving me a sympathetic smile. Apparently, she had got a pretty good idea of what Uncle Charlie was like from their brief talk together.

After thanking the psychic and paying her, I walked her to the front door and saw Shirley hurrying up the front drive. The two women nodded to each other, and then Shirley burst into the hallway.

"I just saw my Uncle Charlie come out your door and walk down the front steps," Shirley said, her face pale with shock. "He disappeared when he reached the sidewalk. Was he the one haunting your house?"

I told Shirley what the psychic had said and about the pinch Uncle Charlie had given me just before he left the house. For the first time since we'd met, Shirley was speechless.

I laughed suddenly and got up. "It will be nice to have my house to myself again," I told her, "although I'm glad I finally got to meet your Uncle Charlie!"

My remark set Shirley off, and we laughed ourselves silly before making our way into the kitchen to brew a pot of herbal tea.

4

A Father's Revenge

DETROIT

He watched uneasily as his only child—a fair daughter—laughed as she traded goods with the handsome white trapper who came to their village each week with his skins. His girl-child was very shy and spoke little even to the people she had known all her life. But now she was glowing as she exchanged soft words with the white man with fair hair and sky-blue eyes. The father did not like what he saw, but what could he say? His daughter did nothing wrong, said nothing unseemly. She just smiled a little too brightly at the trapper's wit and charm as they traded goods.

When the young man was gone, he asked his daughter about her conversation with the white man. What topic had fascinated her so? She turned her bright eyes on her old father, who was chief of his village and whom she loved with her whole heart. "We spoke about life," she said, "about the sun and the stars and the many beautiful things that surround us."

The old chief knew in that moment that his only child was in love with the white man. He knew there was nothing he could say that would change the desire in her heart, so he just touched her cheek gently and walked away. But he did not hold himself as proudly as before, and his sloping shoulders revealed his worry to those who knew him well. His daughter might once have noticed such a change, but now there were stars in her eyes, and she saw nothing but a vision of the handsome face and supple form of the young trapper.

The old chief knew that the young couple was meeting in the meadow outside the village, spending many days walking in the woods and talking. His daughter did not neglect her duties to her father during this time. His meals were served on time, and his clothing was kept clean. But the girl went about her daily tasks with a distracted air, and the old chief knew she was eager to finish her work so she could go to the meadow and see her love.

One day he said to his only daughter, "My child, I will lose you soon, I think."

His daughter blushed happily and nodded. "Yes, father. We were going to ask you for permission to marry as soon as possible. Thomas wants both you and the priest to marry us, so we are bound both by our laws and his."

The old chief nodded, pleased by this news. So the young trapper was serious. Thomas would not take his only daughter as a plaything, but would give her the rank and status she deserved.

"You see," his daughter said playfully. "You should not have worried."

The chief smiled and told his daughter to bring her young man to meet with him the next time Thomas came to the village. She promised this gladly and hummed as she cleared away his meal.

The next morning, the old chief was passing through the wood beside the meadow when he heard his daughter's voice raised in protest. He picked up his pace in alarm, and then stopped when he heard the young trapper's voice.

"Father Constantine said it would be a sin for us to marry," Thomas repeated. "I told him that you would join the church, but he said it did not matter. He said no one will accept us or our children because I am white and you are not."

"You told me that your God was not a white man," the girl replied. "That the one you worship lived and died in a land far across the sea, where men's skins are as dark as mine. If this is so, how can your God look down upon one such as I?"

The trapper would not listen. He repeated Father Constantine's words until the girl was silenced. The old chief trembled with rage, his anger directed more at the friar who had counseled the troubled boy than against the boy himself. He wanted to shake the lad, to tell Thomas to follow his heart and not the words of the priest, but the old chief knew that it was not his place. He had not interfered with the beginning of his daughter's romance, and he would not interfere with its end.

"I am sorry," he heard Thomas saying over and over, as his daughter began to weep. "I am sorry."

The old chief could not bear to hear his daughter crying, and so he moved silently away, returning to his home by another route so his daughter would not see him.

Later, his daughter came into their home silently; her head averted, she made his meal without once looking at him. His heart was wrung with pain at the sight of her grief, and finally he spoke. "Speak to me, daughter," he said. "Tell me what troubles you."

"Thomas is going away," she said, addressing her words to the fire. "We will not be married after all."

"My poor child," the old chief said quietly, his voice choking on the words.

His daughter nodded in acknowledgment, but she did not speak again.

When the old chief woke the next morning, the fire had gone out and there was no sign of his daughter. He sat up abruptly, his heart pounding in fear, and then ran out into the village, clothing askew and hair awry, to search for her. He turned his feet at last toward the river, and then stopped when he saw a huddle of people at the top of the incline, looking down into the pool below. They glanced up when they heard his running feet and then turned away, unable to meet his eyes. He went to the top of the slope and looked down at the slight figure floating face down in the water, her long, dark hair swirling softly around her drowned form.

The old chief did not feel himself fall to his knees; nor was he aware of screaming his daughter's name over and over in agony. He saw nothing save the vision of his child's body drifting there in the water. It was his oldest friend who finally pulled him to his feet and helped him back to his home.

From that moment forward, the only thought in the old chief's mind was that of revenge. He wanted to kill the young trapper who had driven his child to her death, but Thomas had already set out for the East, never to return. So the old chief's hatred turned instead to Father Constantine.

The old chief wasted no time. That night he crept into the friar's room and silently slid a knife into the man's heart. His presence at the fort passed unnoticed, and Father Constantine's body was not discovered until noon of the following day. The whole fort was shocked. The guards were doubled and trebled, but no one knew who killed the good Father, or why.

For a few days, the old chief was at peace. Although he mourned his daughter and turned his duties over to a young cousin who would one day soon be chief, he relished the thought that he had avenged his daughter's death. But gradually, the old chief became aware of a voice calling to him in the wind. Over and over, it spoke his name reproachfully. Finally, the chief recognized the voice of Father Constantine.

"Why did you kill me?" the voice whispered through the treetops during the early evening hours. "Murderer!" it shrieked at the height of a windstorm. The old chief did his best to ignore the voice, chanting prayers and meditating, but the voice only grew louder and more persistent.

"Why did you kill me?" the wind whistled under his blanket at night. "Murderer!" it shouted through the meadow grasses at noon.

Then the tolling of the bells began. *Bong. Bong. Bong.* These were the great bells of the fort, which called the white men to Mass each week. *Bong. Bong. Bong.* But it was the wrong day and the wrong time for Mass. The old chief was confused, and he asked his young cousin why the bells were ringing. His cousin looked at him strangely and very gently told the old chief that no bells had sounded that day.

Still, the old chief heard them ringing, hour after hour, ringing in counterpoint to the voice in the wind shrieking, "Murderer! Murderer!"

Unable to eat, unable to sleep, the old chief sat beside a blackened fire, wrapped in a dirty blanket, shaking and rocking and humming to himself to drown out the voices and the tolling of the bells. Hour after hour his people tried to speak to him, to comfort him, but he was beyond their reach. Still, they loved their old chief, and so all the women and many of the men in the tribe took turns sitting with him, trying to tempt him back to life with delicious food and soft conversation.

The chief sat in silent agony for a week. Then on Sunday morning, the real bells of Mass began to toll. At the sound, the old chief abruptly stopped rocking. He sat up straight and stared into the face of his cousin's wife, whose countenance he saw clearly for the first time in days.

"Tell my cousin to be a good chief," he said to the woman. Then he rose, threw off his blanket, and started running toward the fort. His people called out in amazement and followed him, but he ran with supernatural speed and quickly outdistanced them.

As the last toll of the final bell faded into silence, the old chief burst through the doors of the church and ran straight up to the altar. Tall and proud and angry, he turned to face the congregation. "It was I who killed Father Constantine," he said. "I stole into your fort in the night and took his life because he stole the life of my child, my only daughter! It was he who sent her lover away because her skin was not white; and so she took her own life because of the friar's false counsel. Father Constantine was no better than a murderer, and so I punished him for his crime!"

The old chief stopped abruptly, overcome suddenly with weakness and a terrible pain in his left arm. He stood swaying in agony as the congregation exclaimed in horror. Several soldiers who were attending the early Mass leapt to their feet and approached him cautiously.

A FATHER'S REVENGE

Ignoring them, the old chief turned to look at the priest who had come to replace Father Constantine. "I, too, am a murderer," the old chief said, "and I deserve to die because I took the life of a holy man. I realize this now."

The priest stared down at him, shock and pity on his gentle, intelligent face.

"Pray for me," the old chief whispered to the priest as he fell slowly to the floor of the church. By the time the soldiers reached him, he was dead.

5

The Green Lantern

The storm blew up out of nowhere that night as the ship approached the Green Bay of Lake Michigan. The lookout hung grimly onto the swaying, rain-soaked platform, straining his eyes against the whipping wet wind. He searched the thunderous night, desperately seeking the brightness of the St. Martin Lighthouse on the northeastern side of the island, 18 miles from the tip of the Door County Peninsula. But nothing pierced the darkness save an occasional flash of lightning that lit up the huge waves and sparkled eerily on the driving rain that had soaked the beleaguered sailors straining to keep the schooner on course.

Abruptly, the headlong journey of the ship ceased, and a mighty crash threw the lookout down toward the deck. Only a chance grip on a swinging rope saved him as the ship ground against a shoal and tilted sideways. Below his swinging figure, the monstrous waves continued to crash against the schooner as several members of the crew scrambled to untangle their shipmate. The rest frantically began unhooking the yawls, even before the captain gave the order to abandon ship.

In the dark wretchedness of the storm, no light gleamed. None of the crew knew where the gale had cast them, and they feared for their lives as they struck out onto the tumultuous lake. Giant waves quickly overwhelmed the yawls, and no amount of bailing kept out the water as the crew pulled away from the battered and rapidly breaking hull of the schooner. The men knew that they were doomed, but they kept pushing their way forward, lost and directionless in the storm, until their yawls capsized suddenly, throwing them into the swirling, freezing-cold waves.

"Swim for shore," the lookout shouted suddenly, waving an arm frantically in the darkness and pointing. A greenish light that flickered in the manner of a small lantern pierced the darkness a little south of the sailors. The gleam was weak and hard to see in the storm-ravaged darkness, but it gave them a direction at last. The captain shouted for the men to swim toward the light. The sailors flung themselves forward through the immense waves, sticking together as best they could in the swirling, nightmarish waters.

The flickering green light led them into the shore, and the lookout gave a shout as his feet suddenly touched bottom. Within moments, the rest of the crew joined him and stumbled ashore, looking eagerly for the rescuer who had used his green lantern to guide them to safety. But the beach was empty.

Once again it was the sharp-eyed lookout who spotted the light of a green lantern bobbing ahead of them up a barely visible path. He led the crew forward through a tangle of dark woodland. The men shivered with cold as the storm continued to pummel their soaked bodies. The strain of the wreck and its aftermath caused them to stumble and curse as they followed the lookout and the bobbing green light. Would this nightmare ever end?

Suddenly, the green light increased and then steadied. The crew blinked rapidly, their eyes trying to adjust to the brightness as they left the path. The men entered a small clearing over which loomed the dark lighthouse that had failed to save their ship. The green light was now shining through the half-open door of the keeper's house. The crew hurried through the wind and rain, eager to reach shelter.

The shivering men burst into the house, calling out to the keeper who had guided them to safety. They saw the green lantern standing on the table, its light steady and bright now that it was out of the wind; yet no tall, oilskin-wrapped figure came forward to greet them.

Shutting the door against the raging storm, the captain called again for the lighthouse keeper. No one answered. Then the first mate pointed to a peg on the wall, and the men turned to see a pair of dry oilskins hanging from it. The captain's eyes widened. How could they be dry after such a terrible downpour? Did the lighthouse keeper have a second pair?

Then the lookout called to them from the keeper's bedroom. His voice was high-pitched and strange. The crew exchanged uneasy glances and went into the room. Lying on the bed was the body of the lighthouse keeper. It was obvious that he had been dead for several days, which explained the burned-out light in the tower above them. It did not explain who—or what—had saved them from drowning in the storm.

The crew searched the place thoroughly, but no one else was there. It was the lookout who remembered a story he had heard

THE GREEN LANTERN

about a phantom lighthouse keeper who walked the shores of St. Martin's Island. He related the story to the other men.

There once was a lighthouse keeper who had lived on the island with his children, whom he loved dearly. They were all alone there, for his wife had died long before. Wanting the best for his daughter and son, the keeper had insisted that they continue their education, and for this purpose had purchased a small dory for them, which they rowed across to the mainland each day to attend school. One spring, the children were rowing home from school when they were caught in a sudden squall. Their rowboat overturned and the children were thrown into the depths of the lake. Their bodies were never recovered.

The shattered father searched the beaches of St. Martin's Island every night for the rest of his life, hoping to find his children.

After his death, people started seeing the light of a green lantern moving along the beaches of St. Martin just before a storm. Some folks said it was the spirit of the dead lighthouse keeper continuing his search. Others claimed that the phantom was still on duty, using his lantern to guide ships to safety so their crews would not share the fate of his poor little children.

"It must have been the ghost who led us to safety," the lookout concluded when he finished his tale. The rest of the crew laughed and told him he'd taken one too many knocks to his head during the gale.

The crew revised their opinion the next morning, when the storm had passed and they could search the island for their rescuer. To their consternation, the men discovered that they were completely alone on the island save for the corpse of the long-dead lighthouse keeper. The men could find no explanation for their unexpected rescue except the one offered by the lookout.

On the official records, it was stated that the current lighthouse keeper had died while rescuing the ship's company. The sailors confided the truth to only a few crusty old sea captains who themselves had experienced many mysterious happenings on the Great Lakes and were unlikely to scoff at their tale. After all, who in their right mind would believe that it was a ghost who had saved the lives of the crew on that dark and stormy night?

6

The Ada Witch

GRAND RAPIDS

I'd spent the day hunting in the marshlands around Ada, just a few miles away from my Grand Rapids home, but my luck had run out and I hadn't bagged a thing all day. I'm a little stubborn (my wife would say a lot), so I kept going until it was nearly dark. When the light grew so dim I could barely see the gun in my hand, I knew it was time to quit. Besides, I was cold, my feet were wet, and the owls were hooting at me in annoyance for invading their territory.

"I'm going already," I told the shadowy figure of a barn owl that was glaring at me in the moonlight. "Keep your tail on!" The owl blinked at me and turned its head right around on its neck. *Just what I need, a cocky bird,* I fumed. It was too bad I wasn't hunting owls.

I'd worked this particular area a few times before and I knew the general lay of the land; plus a full moon overhead made the going much easier than it might have been otherwise. Still, as I picked my way through the rugged terrain, I began to feel uneasy. For some reason, it seemed as though someone were watching me from the dark shadows that lined the deep hollows among the trees. I was normally not a believer in the supernatural, but tonight was different. The air was much too chilly for summer, and the skin on my neck and shoulders was prickling in a most unpleasant way. *Shake it off,* I told myself sternly as I made my way across a burbling stream.

Suddenly, I heard the terrified scream of a woman coming from ahead and a little to my right. It sounded as though she was being attacked. Tightening my grip on my rifle, I barreled ahead toward the sound, determined to come to her rescue. As I drew closer, I heard shouts of rage and the sounds of a woman begging for mercy.

I erupted into a clearing, gun in hand, and saw two men struggling desperately with each other. One had a knife, which had obviously been used, as both men were bleeding profusely. To my left, a dark-haired young woman lay on the ground, her dress covered with blood. I gasped at the sight and threw myself between her and the struggling men. I couldn't tell if she was still alive, but I wasn't taking any chances.

I aimed my rifle at the fighters and shouted at them to stop immediately or I would shoot. They ignored me. *Very well, then.* I aimed my gun at the ground near their feet and let off a couple of shots. The men continued to grapple with each other, oblivious to everything save each other. Deciding that stopping them was hopeless, I eased myself back toward the woman, keeping a sharp eye on the men, and sank down next to her to see what I could do to help. She gazed up at me with fathomless eyes that did not register my presence. Her beautiful face was twisted with pain, and I knew she was dying of her wounds.

"I'll get you out of here," I told her, although I didn't believe my own words. She looked too far gone to be moved safely. Keeping one eye on the struggling men, I reached down to help the dying woman to her feet. As I did so, the taller of the two chaps stabbed out with the knife, striking a fatal blow to his opponent's heart. The man sank to his knees and fell face down in the grass. The knife-wielding man gasped a few times and then flopped over backward in a dead faint. Good. That left me free to escape with the injured woman.

I looked back down into her lovely face and slipped my hand under her shoulders. To my horror and amazement, my hand went right through her body! I was pierced by a blood-numbing chill, and my heart began thundering in my chest. Below me, the ethereal woman gave a gasp and a shudder, and then she died, her head falling back and her eyes going completely blank. I stared at her for a moment, and then she disappeared, and with her went the figures of the collapsed men. The moonlit night seemed darker all at once, and I knelt in the grass and dirt too stunned to move. A deep terror gripped me, and I began to shudder uncontrollably.

I don't remember getting up or starting to run. My next memory was of crashing through a bramble thicket and out onto the road where I had parked my car. Fortunately, I had remembered to bring my rifle, because there was no way on earth that I would have gone back to the clearing for it. My hands were shaking so badly that it took me three tries to unlock the car, and another two to get it started. When I finally did, I roared down the road and sped all the way home. I was lucky I didn't get pulled over by the police.

As soon as I came through the door to my house, my wife knew something was wrong. She pried the rifle out of my hands, thrust me into a chair, and got me something hot to drink.

THE ADA WITCH

Then she hovered over me, rubbing my shoulders comfortingly until the involuntary shudders shaking me from head to foot slowed and then ceased.

I didn't think she would believe my story—I hardly believed it myself—but I told her anyway. She listened intently, saying little, but there was no disbelief in her hazel eyes, for which I was grateful.

"It must have been the Ada Witch you saw," she said when I concluded my story. I blinked at her in bewilderment. I was fairly new to the Grand Rapids region, having grown up in Ann Arbor, and I had never heard of the Ada Witch. My wife had lived in this area all her life, and so she told me the story.

Once, long ago, a married Ada woman had taken a lover and had started meeting him in a clearing in the woods near her home. One day, her husband chanced upon the lovers' tryst and attacked the couple in a jealous rage. He killed his wife with a knife, but her lover had fought back fiercely, and the husband wound up receiving as many wounds as the man he was trying to kill. The two men had finally fallen to the ground, overcome by their injuries. One man died instantly, while the other lingered for a few weeks before succumbing to his wounds. But their spirits continued to haunt the area, as did that of the bewitchingly beautiful woman who had ensnared them both.

Residents dubbed the woman's ghost the "Ada Witch," and they claimed that her spirit still roamed the woods at night. People sometimes saw reenactments of the terrible murder in the clearing where it had occurred on nights when the moon was full.

My shudders returned when my wife told me about the ghostly reenactments of the murder, but I'm a pretty tough guy, so I forced them away. Finally, I gave my wife a feeble grin. "I think maybe I'll find another place to go hunting," I said.

My wife chuckled and gave me a big hug.

"That sounds like a good plan," she said.

I never went hunting in the woods near Ada again.

7

The Talking Head

SAULT SAINTE MARIE

There once lived a hunter who was so devoted to his trade that he was almost never home with his wife and two sons. The hunter had not chosen wisely when he took a wife, and his head was so full of the chase and the kill that he did not notice that she was fretful and nagging and completely unfaithful to him. All day long, the wife would talk, talk, talk to her sons and yak, yak, yak with the neighbors and nag, nag, nag at her husband when he came home for a precious few minutes at the end of the hunt.

The unfaithful wife had a series of male "friends" who came to visit her at the lodge, and she instructed her young boys never to speak of these men to their father. At first, the boys were too little to understand what was going on. But as they grew older, they became both horrified and embarrassed by their mother's outrageous behavior.

"I am tired of her talking and nagging and complaining," the elder boy said to his brother. "I am going to speak to Father about her behavior." And his younger brother agreed.

That night when the hunter came home, his eldest boy took him aside while the unfaithful wife was outside talking loudly with their neighbor, and told him the whole story. When the wife returned to the lodge, her nagging voice preceding her by several yards, the hunter confronted her in righteous indignation and struck her dead where she stood.

And that was the end of that. The boy's paternal aunt came to live with them, and things at the lodge became peaceful for about a fortnight. Then their mother returned. Her voice woke the hunter and his boys in the middle of the night. Even before the mother's spirit materialized, they could hear her talk, talk, talking away as fast as she could. Moments later, she was standing at the center of the lodge, shaking her head at the pretty young aunt who was caring for her sons.

The aunt trembled near the door as the glowing figure of the wife began to nag, nag, nag about the cleanliness of the lodge, the shoddy way she dressed the boys, the shameful condition of the blankets and dishes. The ghost went on and on until the hunter was forced to leave the lodge just to get enough sleep to hunt on the morrow. The boys and their aunt were not so lucky; they had to endure the ghostly mother's presence until the spirit grew bored and went to visit the neighbor's lodge.

Each night, the spirit of the mother returned to talk, talk, talk to her sons and yak, yak, yak with the neighbors and nag, nag, nag at her husband and his young sister. It was hard to believe, but she was actually worse in death than she had been in life, and she became a source of intense irritation to the whole village. Nothing the hunter tried could rid his lodge of her incessantly prattling presence. Even the local medicine man gave up after unsuccessfully attempting to exorcise their village of her tiresome spirit.

Finally, everyone in the village packed up their belongings and left. The medicine man nicely but firmly told the hunter and his boys to move somewhere far away from the tribe and to take the spirit with them. The pretty young aunt patted each of them on the hand and then departed with the medicine man, who had decided a virtuous woman that could put up for so long with such a tiresome spirit was good material for a wife.

The hunter and his sons went south, hoping to leave the unwelcome spirit of the yakkety-yakking mother far behind. After traveling for many hours, the hunter left the boys to rest beside a large waterfall while he tracked down some game for their evening meal. The boys stood watching the flight of a beautiful crane that was riding on the surface of the whirling, eddying water at the bottom of the falls. Suddenly, they heard a thump, thump, thumping noise coming from behind them. They turned and saw the grisly remains of their mother's head rolling toward them, her nag, nag, nagging voice shouting loudly to be heard over the noise of the waterfall.

The younger boy stared in terror at the horrible, decaying head and then shouted down toward the crane: "Grandfather Crane! Grandfather Crane! We are being followed by a terrible monster! Please take us across the falls."

The beautiful crane looked up from its play. Seeing their predicament, it flew up to the boys and landed beside them.

"Cling to my back," it told them, "but do not touch my head." The boys nodded obediently, and the crane took them up on its back and flew them across to the far shore.

The head of the dead mother screamed with outrage and nag, nag, nagged at the crane to take it across to her sons.

THE TALKING HEAD

"Come, Grandfather," the talking head shouted. "Carry me across the waterfall to my poor, lost children!"

Across the river, the boys watched with apprehension as the crane flew to the grisly, rotting head and said, "Cling to my back, but do not touch my head." The mother's head promised obedience and bounced up onto the crane's back. But the mother's spirit was as indiscreet in life as it had been in death. It was curious to know why the crane did not want its head touched. When they were about halfway across the waterfall, it bumped itself forward and tapped the crane on the head. Immediately, the crane twisted and lurched in distress and the talking head tumbled off its back and fell screaming into the roaring water below.

The head was swept against the sharp rocks, and the rotting brains burst forth from the demolished skull and flew out over the water. The crane banked and flew down toward the battered remains of the mother's head. "You were useless in life," it cried loudly. "You will not be useless in death! Become fish."

Immediately, the floating pieces of brain transformed into fish eggs, which, when hatched, grew into a delicate, flavorful whitefish that became very popular in the region. Thus was the nag, nag, nagging spirit destroyed forever, and the young boys saved from persecution.

When the hunter, upon his return, heard the boys' terrifying tale, he praised the crafty grandfather crane and adopted it as his family totem. The hunter and his sons settled down in the place that became known as Sault Sainte Marie, and their descendants became great hunters and fishermen who ate numerous whitefish and always rejoiced in the flight of the crane.

8

The Staircase

GRAND HAVEN

It felt as if he had been climbing the staircase forever. First one dragging step and then another, up and up. The stairs were old and crumbling. There was a groove worn in the middle of each one, as if many people had walked this way before.

The light around him was dim—always dim; it was hard to see his surroundings. The air was fresh, and there was the faintest breath of wind against his cheeks. Gray trees and bushes seemed to press in on the staircase from either side. He could make out nothing else save this infernal staircase stretching up and up as far as his eye could see.

He wished that he could remember why he was climbing the stairs—or when he started, or how he got here. If he was honest with himself—something he refrained from doing whenever possible—he even wished he could remember who he was.

He dodged that thought, or tried to, burying himself in the task at hand. Keep climbing. Don't stop. Lift one foot, then the next. Ignore the drag of gravity. Ignore the red-hot thigh muscles and the tension in the lower back. Just climb.

But it didn't help. His unknown identity teased him from the edge of consciousness. And he did not like what he saw; not one bit. Something about this endless climb, this dim light, the oddly fresh air with its hint of foreign spices was forcing him to face honesty for the first time since early childhood. His mind shied away from that honesty, but the staircase wouldn't let him hide from himself. Not anymore.

Climb, he told himself, just climb. But inside his mind, he saw the shining, innocent face he presented to his teachers when he denied all knowledge of why his classmate's arms were so badly bruised she couldn't hold her books. They thought her father must be hitting her, and they made a lot of trouble for that family. No one believed that a little boy could be hurting her, and the girl was too afraid to speak up. Eventually, the family packed their belongings and moved away.

He shied away at the memory of the girl's fear, though it had never bothered him before. In fact, he had secretly gloated over it, wishing he could make his brilliant little sister—whom his parents idolized—look at him with the same fear. He hated her; he hated her and he could not touch her. His parents divorced when he was in the sixth grade, and his mother and sister moved far away. Yet she was the one his father always talked about, boasted about, was proud of.

Climb, he told himself, wiping the sweat from his forehead and pushing the wretched thoughts away. Just climb.

The gray trees loomed around him, and he thought he caught glimpses of his sister's face in their shadows. The wind rustled through the leaves, and he heard his sister's mocking voice in the sound. She had teased him ruthlessly for being so "dumb." For getting average grades. For not being very good at sports.

He pushed himself, mounting the staircase as fast as he could to avoid the buried memories, keeping his eyes on the grooves in each worn stair. Once he clapped his hands over his ears to shut out his little sister's mocking voice. He was the elder, but she was the better! Her theme song from the moment she could talk.

The wind died down suddenly, and his sister's voice faded. When he dared glance at the gray trees, all he saw was gnarled bark. He slowed his steps, the muscles of his legs screaming in agony. He had to rest. There was no landing in sight, so he sat down on the staircase itself. It felt cool and pleasant to his touch, and his legs trembled with exhaustion as he stretched them. Would this wretched climb never end? he wondered, peering into the dimness surrounding him. Would he never make it to the top?

He drew in a calming breath, and with it came another memory: another face from his unknown past. Another girl staring at him in terror. He leapt abruptly to his feet and started climbing again, thrusting the memory away. Somehow, in this dim light, he saw her terror for what it was, and it no longer gave him pleasure. Quite the reverse. The girl's screams for mercy followed him as he stumbled upward.

The wind rose around him, and now he heard the voices of all his victims, screaming in anger and pleading, pleading, pleading with him to stop. Some prayed. Some wept. He howled aloud himself, running upward with his hands clapped over his ears, trying to blot out the voices. In the gray woods, he now saw the girls and women he had killed, their spirits hovering just above the ground, fingers pointed, eyes judging, mouths open to condemn. Not helpless now. They were coming for him! He had to reach the top of the staircase before they reached him.

His soul writhed within him, and the guilt he had never felt before overwhelmed him all at once. He screamed again and fled upward as fast as his legs could carry him, his body slumped almost in half as he tried to bear the horrible pain radiating out from his gut, from his chest, from his mind.

The stairs above his head seemed brighter suddenly, and his heart thundered with hope. It was the top of the staircase. He was almost out of this terrible place. Almost out!

Above him, radiant light suddenly burst forth as if someone had opened a door, and he slowed on the steps and then stopped. The light swirled and pulsed like a living thing, and in its brilliance he suddenly saw himself clearly for the very first time. In that blinding moment, he knew himself as others knew him, and he wanted to die. He was a perverted, filthy, worthless creature with no goodness anywhere in his being. He tried to scream, but nothing came out of his throat.

And then he saw her, his little sister, descending the staircase toward him. She appeared as she had when he last saw her alive, her body broken and bleeding, her face bruised beyond recognition. He had triumphed at her downfall, but now the sight of her made him tremble with agony, with remorse; all the gloating hatred he had felt when he killed her—his final victim— melted away before the look in her eyes as she descended toward him in the gloriously radiant light.

She held out a hand toward him and he backed away, stumbling down the stairs. She said something, but he did not hear her words. He had turned now and was running, running, running back down the staircase, unable to face her. He deserved

THE STAIRCASE

her condemnation, deserved every hard thing she had ever said to him in life. But that was not what sent him flying away from her.

In that final moment, he feared something even worse than her condemnation; he feared her forgiveness, and he *could not* live with that. He was her murderer. And not just that. He was a serial killer who had stalked any girl or woman who reminded him of his sister. There could be no forgiveness for him. Not from her. Not from God. Not from anyone. And certainly never from himself.

He ran stooped over, stumbling down a staircase which no longer seemed to go on forever. It seemed short. Too short. He could already see the bottom, and the gaping red-hot doorway rimed with brimstone and fire that awaited him. His victims lined the staircase on either side, standing tall and triumphant as he raced past them toward the door. The very last one in line was his little sister, and their eyes met once just before he stepped through the door.

9

The Merchant

The sailor had hightailed it out of Bay City on the first ship he could find—which was an old schooner barge called the *Comrade*. He left behind an unfaithful wife and her lover, both rather the worse for wear after he discovered them together and tossed the love-struck man out of their bedroom window— their second-floor bedroom window, that is.

The sailor thought it best to make himself scarce before his wife could complain to the police, so he hurried down to the docks to look for a ship. The *Comrade* was in-tow to a steamer called the *Columbia*, and neither ship was in good shape. But the sailor figured anything was better than jail, and so he joined the crew, taking watches and doing his duty while keeping his head down and staying quiet.

The trip north to Ashland went without a hitch, and they were heading back toward Cleveland, steaming past the Keweenaw Peninsula, when a heck-of-a-large southwester came roaring out of Lake Superior, churning up the water and blowing everything to kingdom come. Massive waves the size of houses buffeted both ships, and it wasn't long before the hawser tying them together came loose and the *Comrade* was set adrift.

51

There was no way the *Columbia* could retrieve the schooner barge in that mighty storm, and her captain wasn't fool enough to try.

The sailor had been on the lakes since he was a lad of ten, but never had he seen such a storm. Without the *Columbia* to help them, he figured they were all doomed. He was just glad he'd had the opportunity to throw his wife's lover out the window before he went to meet his Maker.

The barge rolled from one side to the other in the thrashing waves. It sank lower and lower, until suddenly it fell out from under the sailor's feet and he found himself fighting for his life beneath the water, kicking and struggling against the massive undertow caused by the sinking ship and swimming for the only marginally lighter water near the surface. His head broke through at last, and he gasped for breath, treading water and trying to see in the midnight-darkness of the storm.

The sailor was in the trough of a giant wave when he emerged from the depths, and it wasn't until he reached the next peak that he saw the yawl only a few yards from him. He struck out immediately for the small sailboat, the only thing left from the *Comrade*, and dragged himself aboard. The sails were tattered to bits, and the sailor didn't even try to steer. He just hung on for dear life as the storm bellowed and raged around his shivering, soaking-wet body.

He was lucky it was summertime, or he would have died of exposure and cold before the storm rumbled away. The tumult was followed by an eerie calm, and a thick fog worthy of merry old England. The sailor shivered and snuffled and rubbed his arms to keep out the cold, wondering where the yawl was taking him. Suddenly, a huge black shadow loomed through the fog, and he heard a voice: "Ahoy there, the yawl! Do you need help?"

The sailor blinked in bewilderment, roused himself from his stupor, and shouted a reply. Within a few moments, he found himself being hauled up onto a big, old-fashioned, top-masted schooner, and his yawl taken in tow behind the ship. In a daze, he was shuffled kindly into the foc'c'sle and given clean, dry clothes. The cook brought him a thick, rich stew that heated up his insides and made him drowsy. He was asleep before he lay down in the bunk they made up for him, and he didn't wake until late the next day.

The sailor was welcomed gladly by captain, crew, and passengers. He soon learned that he was on a schooner called the *Merchant*, bound for Eagle Harbor on the Keweenaw Peninsula. The ship was carrying a load of mining equipment; strange cargo to the sailor's mind, since the Keweenaw hadn't been actively mined for many years. Several of the passengers claimed to be miners, and their rough clothing and hearty manner seemed to substantiate their claim. There were also a few lumberjacks on board, and one soldier. The sailor thought it odd to find a soldier aboard the ship in these peaceful times, but he was in no mood to worry. He was too busy feeling grateful to be alive.

The passengers took turns talking to the sailor, demanding details about the shipwreck and particulars about his home. One old fellow wanted to know what year it was and who was president. This question baffled the sailor, and he began to wonder why the passengers seemed so disconnected to the present.

Overhead, the sky was blue, and the wind whistled cleanly through the air, filling the sails of the *Merchant*. They were making very good time. As the sailor relaxed, ate, and chatted with the passengers, the ship sailed on and on and on, moving ceaselessly toward the wide horizon.

It was around noon on the third day that it finally dawned on the sailor that something was wrong. It should have taken them no more than a day, by his reckoning, to reach port. So why were they still sailing? The ship was traveling the right direction and seemed to be moving briskly. But no land was in sight. And no one else seemed to have noticed their lack of progress.

Uneasy, the sailor started watching the crew and passengers as he made his way around the ship. He noted, as he had when he first arrived onboard, that their speech was old-fashioned, and their clothing out of date. Now it dawned on the sailor that—aside from the day they pulled him aboard—he had never heard the passengers discussing the world outside the ship, or what they intended to do when they disembarked. They acted as if they never expected to leave the *Merchant*; as if the ship were their whole world.

That night, the sailor woke from a terrible nightmare. In his dream, he was chained up in the darkest hold of the ship, never more to see the light of day. He had faded away there, until he was nothing but a ghostly voice calling for the crew to let him out. As the sailor bolt upright in bed, shaking with fear, he suddenly remembered a story an ancient mariner had once told him about a schooner called the *Merchant* which left the Soo one clear day in 1847. The ship was bound for Keweenaw Peninsula and was carrying supplies for the mines that were still

THE MERCHANT

active at that time. But the ship never made her destination, and she was presumed lost somewhere on Lake Superior.

The sailor shivered, realizing only then that he was sheltering aboard a ghost ship, doomed to sail on forever, never reaching her destination. He wondered if he himself were dead. He thought not; but he might as well be, he decided, if he stayed aboard the *Merchant*.

The sailor slipped silently from his bunk, careful not to disturb the sleeping passengers who shared his room, and crept cautiously up on deck. Avoiding the night watch, he made his way down to his yawl, released it from its mooring, and slipped inside. As soon as he was free of the wake of the schooner, he began rowing for shore with all his strength, guiding himself by the stars. After an hour, the wind blew up from the north and sent the yawl careening toward the distant land. The water became so choppy that the sailor could do nothing but hang on and hope for the best. Toward dawn, he saw the coastline appear on the horizon. And a few hours later, the yawl capsized in the surf at the shoreline, and the sailor dragged himself onto the beach.

After resting, the sailor hiked inland until he found railroad tracks. He followed them until he was overtaken by a lumber train. He hitched a ride on the last car, and soon the train rolled into Marquette. Realizing that he still had his wallet, the sailor walked into the local tavern, ordered food and drink, and struck up a conversation with a captain taking shore leave. Working the conversation around to local events, the sailor learned to his horror that the *Comrade* had been lost—presumably with all of its hands—in a storm three months previous. What had seemed to the sailor a three-day journey on the ghost ship had actually taken three months! It would not have taken long for him to die of old age at that rate.

Thankful to have escaped, the sailor secured a berth on the captain's ship under an assumed name, remembering just in time that he was a wanted man in Bay City. Since he was presumed dead, the sailor figured he'd better stay dead for the duration, rather than risk a jail cell down the road.

The sailor never saw the ghost ship again, though he often thought about the poor *Merchant* and her crew, doomed to sail forever toward the Keweenaw Peninsula without ever reaching their destination.

10

Ghost Train

TAHQUAMENON FALLS STATE PARK

Well, ol' Con Culhane was just about the roughest, toughest lumber boss in the north woods. He'd lick a man before he'd hire him, and any man who could stand up to him was guaranteed a job and a good salary to boot. One fellow I heard about licked the boss fair and square, and Con hired him on as a "straw boss," which is what we lumberjacks call a worker who acts as a boss or crew leader in addition to performing regular duties.

Con was lumbering the white pine in the regions around Sheldrake in those days, and I was one of his straw bosses. We kept the men in line and the lumber moving. There were only a few men—and one woman—whom Con really respected, and I was one of them. The woman was his wife, Ellen, who kept the books and made sure the business ran at a profit. Ellen was the power behind the big, blustering Irishman.

Well, as we logged further and further away from Lake Superior, we began finding it difficult to move lumber down to the rivers. It wasn't so bad in midwinter, when we could use sleds for the relatively short run to the riverside banking grounds. But come the spring thaw, things weren't so easy.

Now Con had been closely monitoring the development of the logging railroads to the south. Logging railroads were introduced in the 1850s. Small engines and portable narrow gauge track made it possible for lumberjacks to log farther away from the rivers. The railroads could haul loads of logs no matter what the weather, and in some cases, the river drive itself could be avoided entirely by carrying the logs straight to a mainline railroad depot.

When Con spoke with Ellen about the possibility of starting his own lumber railroad, she was eloquent in her praise. According to his wife, the logging railroad was sufficiently economical to allow cutting in areas that had been considered too far from the nearest driving stream to make sledding practical. Furthermore, railroad tracks could be picked up and relaid through the forest, making them an even better investment.

So Con got his logging railroad. The restless lumberman took a fierce delight in driving the trains, building spurs and short lines, and hauling lumber. Con was tireless in his expansion efforts. One winter he moved his logging equipment and railroad south from the Little Two-Hearted River to the Tahquamenon River valley by laying tracks in front of him as he drove across frozen swamps, then picking them up from behind him as he went.

Con built a railroad bridge right across the Tahquamenon River using not much more than his bare hands and the back-breaking labor of his men. Then he put a chute into the mouth of the Tahquamenon Falls so his logs could ride smoothly to the bottom rather than smashing into the rocky pool at the base of the cliff. No task was too big for Con Culhane. He even dammed the Two-Hearted River so he could use it to drive logs to Lake Superior.

Pretty soon Con could afford to run two locomotives to move the lumber, but his pride and joy was the first train Ellen had bought for her man. Indeed, the logging went so swiftly and penetrated so deeply into the Upper Peninsula that several competing companies packed up and moved to Wisconsin or Minnesota. There just was not much virgin forest left in the area. It seemed that one day soon Con would be forced to make some difficult decisions about what to do with his successful business. But that day never came. Because one afternoon, while working on his beloved railroad, Con fell beneath the wheels of one of his trains and was killed instantly.

We were in shock, the boys and I. No one ever expected the big man to die—he was too hearty and full of life. Things got quiet pretty quickly without Con around. And Ellen lost some of her spirit when she lost her man. But she kept the business running, and we kept moving logs, just like Con always did.

Well, the years passed, our territory got lumbered out, and most of us moved on. But I would sometimes ride up that way to visit the places I'd worked when I was young. The first summer I returned, I was walking near the abandoned location of our first rail yard when I heard the distinct whistle of a logging locomotive. Oh, I knew that whistle. I'd heard it a thousand times when Con Culhane blew it coming into the yard. I whipped around, looking for the source of the sound. But nothing was there. The portable narrow gauge track had been moved out long ago, and nothing had replaced it.

I heard the whistle again, and I followed the sound back into the woods, walking along the overgrown spur that had

GHOST TRAIN

once bustled with lumberjacks, trains, and logs. The whistle blew again a third time. In that moment, I saw the woods the way they used to be; the hustle and bustle of the rail yard and the hurly-burly behavior of the rowdy lumberjacks just coming off duty. The figures around me were shadowy, black and white like the pictures on the new-fangled television set my grandson and his wife have set up in their kitchen.

Whoo! Whoo! The whistle blew a fourth time. Briefly I saw—again, in black and white—Con's first engine, his pride and joy, coming toward me along narrow gauge railroad tracks that were no longer there. The train passed so close to me that I could have touched it, and Con leaned out the window and doffed his cap, just like he used to in the old days when he saw me in the rail yard.

As I waved my hand to my old friend, everything vanished just as suddenly as it had appeared. I shook my head, wondering if I had dreamed the whole thing. Then I hiked back to my car and turned for home. Just before leaving, I stopped by the house of one of the locals whom I had known since childhood. Sheepishly, I asked him if he ever heard the sound of a locomotive running through the woods.

The old man chuckled. "So you've seen Con's train too, have you?"

I nodded slowly.

"No one around these parts talks about it much, but everyone hears the train going by now and then, when Con's in the mood to visit his old stomping grounds," he said. "Mostly, we just hear the whistle blowing."

I thanked him and left in a thoughtful mood, stopping just once during my journey to visit Con Culhane's gravesite so I could to say farewell once more to my good friend.

11

The Phantom Trespasser

SAGINAW

Father was not a man to be trifled with, as we children knew all too well. He was a big rawboned man, with a grizzled head of curly hair and a hearty laugh that could shake the rafters. But he was also a stern disciplinarian, and we learned early on not to cross him. So when a trespasser started roaming 'round our new house and yard, we knew it would not be long before Father decided to do something.

My brothers had seen the dark-haired, wrinkled old man from time to time, wandering near the house. Once I saw him in the kitchen, disappearing through the back door; literally, *through* the door, for it was closed at the time. I decided not to mention that incident to Father. He already thought I was a silly girl with a head full of boys and other nonsense. If I told him our trespasser was from the Other Realm, he would probably send me away to a convent until I was forty!

Aside from the trespasser, our rambling house was pretty normal, with almost enough bedrooms, a cozy kitchen, and a formal parlor downstairs. We even had a library full of books. The library was my favorite room. In spite of what Father said, I was far from an "empty-headed" girl. I was a woman with ambitions, and I planned to attend university, even though that was "not done" by the girls in our social circle. I was in my last year of high school, and I studied nearly as often as I checked my hair in the mirror or daydreamed about Harry, the boy who lived across the street.

I'd met Harry on the day we moved to Saginaw. He was studying to be a doctor, and he was almost my beau. That was another thing I didn't mention to Father, for fear he would shoot right through the roof.

Harry was intrigued when I told him about our phantom. Together, we started asking around our neighborhood to see if there had been any unexpected deaths or tragic happenings connected to our house that might explain the ghost. We struck gold when we went to interview the old woman who lived in the house right behind ours. According to Mrs. Smith, a previous owner had died of heart failure in the front parlor. His name was Mr. Taylor, and he had been obsessed with his house and its grounds.

"Mr. Taylor's spirit comes back to check up on the house every now and again," old Mrs. Smith told me and Harry. "Perhaps you've seen him?" She gave us a knowing smile.

We both nodded eagerly.

"Well, best to leave his ghost alone," Mrs. Smith advised us. "Mr. Taylor had a bad temper, and the neighborhood children took care never to vex him. Once he caught a little fellow picking flowers in his front garden and chased the boy all the way down the block. After that, Mr. Taylor shouted curses at the little boy every time he passed by until the poor little lad was too scared to walk down the block."

"How terrible," I exclaimed, sitting up indignantly. "What happened next?"

"Well," said Mrs. Smith, "the boy worked up his courage and went to the house to apologize to Mr. Taylor for taking his flowers. After that, everything was as right as rain. Mr. Taylor never was one to hold a grudge, I'll give him credit for that."

I settled back in my chair and finished eating the cookies Mrs. Smith had given me and Harry. Mr. Taylor sounded like a tough old man to me, but no more so than my own father. In fact, I suspected I might have liked him, as long as I was careful to stay on his good side. When we were done eating the cookies, Harry and I thanked Mrs. Smith and went home.

That very same day, Father announced at supper that he'd had enough of our trespasser. He loaded up his rifle around 9:00 p.m. and stalked outside into the growing darkness. I watched through the window as he stumbled and cursed his way into the shrubbery to lay in wait for the prowler. I wondered what he would make of the ghostly Mr. Taylor, and what Mr. Taylor would make of him.

I spent the evening peering out of my upper-story window to see how Father was doing (and to watch the light burning in Harry's bedroom window), so I was the first to see the phantom trespasser when he appeared in the garden. Mr. Taylor materialized next to the gate, looking toward the house. As he strolled casually forward, inspecting the well-manicured lawn, Father erupted from the shrubbery with a yell that could have woken the dead. Taking aim with his rifle, Father fired a shot at the phantom. The bullet went right through its translucent body and lodged in a nearby tree. To my surprise, the ghostly

Mr. Taylor stumbled a bit and clutched at his arm, as if the bullet had stung him. He gave Father an angry glare, then he vanished into thin air with a small popping noise like the sound of a cork coming out of a wine bottle.

Inside the house, my mother was exclaiming in fright over the gunshot, and my brothers were cheering and running down the staircase to the front hall. The boys whole-heartedly supported Father's method of dealing with trespassers, and they were at an age that anything having to do with blood and gore appealed to them mightily. I followed my family out onto the porch. To my surprise, I found Harry there, beating the bushes with Father. Harry had come running when he heard the rifle shot, and Father had dragooned him into searching for the man that he'd "winged" with his rifle. Father searched the grounds for nearly an hour, but found no sign of Mr. Taylor. I took Harry aside privately and showed him the tree in which Father's bullet had lodged. We decided not to tell Father that he'd shot a ghost.

The next evening, the phantom trespasser returned with a vengeance. The whole household was awakened from sleep by a thunderous banging on the walls, which moved from one room to the next, upstairs and down, all night long. Father chased the sound around and around, looking rather ludicrous in his long gray nightshirt and cap, a glowing lantern clutched in one hand. Sometimes he rapped the wall right where the spirit was knocking and ordered it to come out and "fight like a man." Between the ghost's antics and Father's shouting, we didn't get much sleep that night.

In the days that followed, the ghostly Mr. Taylor appeared to escort us out of the yard every time any one of us left the house. I didn't mind a bit, since the fellow doffed his hat to me and behaved in a very gentleman-like fashion. He was courteous to Mother too, and he shadow-boxed with my two young brothers, much to their delight. He seemed altogether solid when he was in the shade. It was only when he stepped into bright sunlight that we could see through him. He even bowed to Harry when my beau came home from his summer job. Harry was taken aback at the sight of the phantom, whom he had heard about but never before seen. But he recovered quickly and bowed back politely, remembering what Mrs. Smith had told us about the ghost's fiery temper.

It was a completely different story with Father. As soon as he stepped from the porch, the phantom would appear with a martial light in his eye. He would silently rant at Father and dog his steps out into the street. Father took to peering anxiously through a window before he left the house, and then he'd make for the road at a dead run. His strategy never varied, and it never worked. My brothers and I found the whole situation hilarious, though we smothered our giggles with our hands lest Father hear us and tan our hides for the crime of disrespect. Even Mother's lips twitched when Father began his ritual for leaving the house.

In the hours after supper, we'd gather in the parlor to relax and read. Sometimes the phantom trespasser would join us, though he remained mostly invisible. I could see his hands, which he would teasingly pass between my eyes and book as he passed by my chair with a soft puff of chilly wind. My brothers would exclaim and giggle when he did the same to them, and Father would glare at them for disturbing his reading. A few moments later, Father would shout aloud with annoyance when the ghostly Mr. Taylor played the same joke on him, and Mother would tell him to hush and sit down before he disturbed the neighbors. Though her voice was stern, her eyes twinkled merrily at me once Father returned to reading.

When Father was alone in the parlor, the tricks played by the phantom trespasser accelerated. Newspapers were tweaked out of his hand, the fire in the stove would go out abruptly, or the lights would wink off and on. Father stopped using the parlor altogether unless another family member was with him. And woe-be-it to us if we left the room long enough for the phantom trespasser to pull any tricks.

Nights were particularly trying, because we never knew if we were going to get any sleep. Some nights were peaceful, but others were full of rapping and rumbling and an occasional bang that interrupted our slumber and made Father run around and around in bare feet with his nightcap askew.

News of our ghost had spread through the neighborhood, though it was rare that anyone outside the family could see him, even when he stood directly in front of their noses. Harry could see him, but I believe this was because the phantom knew Harry was my beau and considered him one of the family.

One evening, Father invited a number of his skeptical friends to spend the night in our guest room to experience our ghost firsthand. The phantom trespasser was very obliging that night, whipping newspapers from shaking hands, banging on the walls, and sending the skeptics running for their lives.

The phantom may have enjoyed himself hugely that evening, but Mother had had enough. She confronted Father in the kitchen the next morning right after breakfast. Though my brothers and I listened at the door, we could not make out

THE PHANTOM TRESPASSER

exactly what she said to him in her low, furious voice. Whatever it was, it had an instant effect.

Scowling fiercely, Father marched out the front door, down into the yard, and apologized to the ghost of Mr. Taylor, who had appeared as usual the moment Father's foot touched the front porch. It was a fulsome apology indeed, starting with his inexcusably rude behavior in shooting Mr. Taylor and ending with his subsequent inhospitable and offensive manner. The tone and the words sounded more like those used by Mother, but Father's contrition was sincere, and the phantom trespasser seemed to know it. When Father finished speaking, the ghostly Mr. Taylor grasped his hand and shook it enthusiastically. Then he waved to my brothers and me, who were watching from the porch, and marched down the front walk, vanishing when he reached the road.

I told Harry the whole story when he came over after work. "I'm afraid that's the last we'll see of the phantom trespasser," I said with a sigh. I'd grown fond of our ghost, despite his antics.

"Not necessarily," Harry predicted with a smile.

And he was right. The nocturnal noises and the parlor tricks ceased after Father apologized to Mr. Taylor's ghost. But the phantom trespasser would still occasionally appear in the yard near our house, bowing to Mother and me, shadow-boxing with the boys, and nodding politely to Father, which made me glad.

12

One Last Head

Folks hereabouts were never too fond of the Quick family. Old Man Quick had moved to Michigan territory with his son Billy shortly after the death of his wife. He built a house out back in the woods a long way from the settlement and eked out a living by hunting and trapping. Folks tried to be friendly with Old Man Quick and his boy when they first came to the settlement to sell 'coon skins and buy supplies for the winter. But the hunter and his son weren't much on socializing, and their taciturn ways and rough speech soon turned people against them.

When young Bill turned eighteen, things changed a bit. The lad started coming to some of the town socials, and he even cracked a few jokes with the fellows playing checkers in the mercantile. Then he started courting a nice young lady from a good family. Bill soon won her heart and her hand, and they settled down with Old Man Quick out in the backwoods. Surprisingly enough, the marriage was a happy one, though the girl's parents disapproved of Bill and were upset that their only daughter lived so far away. When the girl died in childbirth, her parents swept down upon the grieving father and took their little grandson away with them before he knew what had happened.

After the death of his wife, Bill grew as taciturn as his father and stopped coming in to town. He rarely saw his son and didn't interfere in his upbringing in any way. Things went on like this for years. Then one day Bill came home to find his father dead on the cabin floor. Old Man Quick had been tomahawked to death and partially scalped by an Indian war party that had raided the lonely cabin while Bill was out checking his traps.

Well, Bill just about went mad with grief and fury. And in the years that followed, Bill became even more reclusive. He came to town only once a year for winter supplies, and he rarely communicated with his son, young Tom Quick, who still lived with his in-laws. Bill Quick's cabin became more and more decrepit. The smell coming from it got to be so bad that passing hunters took to avoiding that patch of the woods altogether, opting to make the long trek to town rather than bunking with Bill for the night.

It was during this period that the relationship between the settlement and the local Pottawatomie and Wyandot tribes became strained. No one knew for sure why the tribesmen became so wary of their white neighbors, or why they stopped trading with the people in town. Eventually they withdrew completely, staying close to their tribal lands and avoiding the white men altogether. Things stayed this way for a long time. As the years passed, the townsfolk almost forgot that the settlement had ever traded with the local tribes.

Tom Quick grew into an easygoing young man who was nothing like his taciturn, reclusive father. He'd been much indulged by his maternal grandmother, and he took to drink and cards rather than hard work and religion. Still, folks preferred him to his father. Bill Quick behaved more and more like a wild man during his infrequent visits to town. There was something about him that frightened even the toughest frontiersmen, and something in his eyes that terrified the womenfolk. They claimed time and again that his pupils gleamed red like those of a maddened beast.

One day, a local hunter passing near Bill Quick's cabin heard a heart-rending wail coming from inside. He went to investigate and found Bill Quick lying on a cot in the main room. Quick begged the hunter to send his son Tom to him before he died, and the compassionate man hurried into town to do as Bill bade him.

Tom was surprised and touched by the summons. He had almost reconciled himself to his father's complete indifference toward him, though he secretly wished that his father would love him, if only a little. He hurried through the woods toward the Quick cabin, hoping to get there before Bill died.

As he entered the clearing where the cabin stood, he was overwhelmed by the stench of rotting meat. Tom gasped and reeled backward, retching and fighting to control his stomach. The smell was far worse than the hunters in town had described. Tom no longer wondered that they avoided the place. He wanted to turn and run—but his father was dying inside that cabin, so he forced himself forward.

He called out to Bill as he knocked on the door, and his father answered from a cot by the closed door in the far wall. The smell was even worse inside the cabin, but Tom steeled himself and stepped into the room. Bill's emaciated, fever-stricken form lay on the bed. His rough face was flushed with fever, and he was picking restlessly at the tattered cover that lay over him. He snapped at his son to come over where he could see him, and Tom walked slowly to his side. The smell was so bad now that he had to concentrate on controlling his stomach. It seemed to be pulsing out from behind the closed door beside his father's cot.

"I'm dying, curse it," Bill began abruptly when Tom reached the bed, "and I won't be able to finish my life's work. So you're going to have to do it."

"What life's work?" Tom asked. This was the first time the old man had ever spoken of such a thing.

"My revenge!" his father shouted, his pupils gleaming red with madness. "My collection!" Bill gestured toward the closed door and told his son to go into the next room.

Trying to breathe only through his mouth, Tom opened the latch and stepped through the door. He was met by a blast of foul air, and he paused in horror as his eyes took in shelf upon shelf of human heads lining every wall of the room. Some were merely skulls; others were half-rotten and crawling with worms and beetles. At least one was nearly fresh, and Tom could still see the look of shock on the face of the Pottawatomie tribesman to whom it had once belonged. There was only one empty space left in the room, at the center of the back wall; a gap just big enough to fit one more head.

"Dear God in heaven!" Tom cried. He backed out of the door, wanting to run but unable to tear his eyes from the grotesque collection.

"Father, what have you done?" he cried, whirling at last to face the dying old man on the cot.

"I have avenged your grandfather," Bill Quick said. "On the day he died, I swore to take the heads of one hundred Indians in exchange for the scalp they took from my father."

As Tom struggled to listen, Bill described how he tracked down his prey, waiting until he found a tribesman hunting alone and then shooting him through the heart. He never needed more than one bullet for each man, he told his son proudly. And he removed each man's head for his grisly collection.

At first, it had been easy to find individual hunters, but the Pottawatomie and Wyandot tribes had become wary as the death toll mounted, and soon none of the men went out hunting alone. But Bill had continued his hunt, stalking his victims ever more carefully, and had continued to add to his terrible collection until this fever had laid him low.

"Ninety-nine heads line my walls," he told his son. "You must kill the last Indian and fulfill my oath to your grandfather."

Fighting to control his revulsion, Tom glared at the figure on the bed and told him that he would have nothing to do with his terrible oath. Bill Quick rose up from his pillow, his eyes red with rage. Tom backed away in horror, afraid that he would become his father's next victim.

"Give me one last head," Bill Quick howled, his voice that of a madman. "One last head!"

Tom ran for the door as fast as his shaking legs would carry him. He fumbled with the latch, hearing the cot creak as his insane father tried to rise. His sweaty palms kept slipping off the metal latch, but finally he got the door open and threw himself into the yard.

The voice of his father followed him as he fled from the Quick cabin: "Fulfill my oath or my spirit will return from the grave to seek you out! One last head!"

Tom ran as far and as fast as he could. When he could run no longer, he flung himself down upon the leaf-strewn dirt and sobbed in fear and rage and revulsion. Time passed; how long, he didn't know. Finally, when all traces of tears and sickness were gone, he went back to the settlement and straight to the pub to drown his sorrow in whisky.

It took several days and many drinks to ease the horror of Tom's meeting with his father. One evening, the hunter who had brought Tom his father's deathbed message came and told him that the old man had died. He'd checked on him that day and found him dead in his cot. The longer he talked, the harder Tom found it to control his countenance as he visualized every sordid corner of the cabin.

"Don't feel bad that he was alone when he passed, son," the hunter said gruffly, reading only grief in Tom's expression. "Ol' Bill preferred it that way."

Tom nodded wordlessly, and the hunter took himself off, privately touched by the depth of feeling Tom had for his crazy old father.

That night, Tom was awakened by the sound of the wind howling outside his window. He sat up in bed and saw a glow coming from the treetops outside. It formed into the face of his father, his eyes glowing red with insanity, his open mouth a fathomless black hole. "One last head!" the apparition shrieked.

Tom screamed in terror and hid underneath his covers until the ghastly face disappeared. Then he jumped out of bed and ran into the main room to get a bottle of whisky, which he speedily emptied. He spent the rest of the night by the fire, his back to the window, refusing to look up from the flames.

Everywhere he turned the next day, Tom saw his dead father. A pair of red eyes watched as he rode away from the farm toward town. An emaciated form appeared on the roof of the mercantile, glaring down on him as he tied his horse to the hitching post. The wind howled through the main street, whipping around him and shrieking "one last head" into his ear. Tom ended up in the tavern, seeking courage in a bottle, and was so drunk by the day's end that he spent the night in the lock-up.

Tom spent more and more of his time that way, since it seemed the only way to avoid the ghost of his father. But drink only muted the terror he felt when he saw his father's specter lurking in the shadows, or felt malevolent red eyes watching him. And soon, even the voices of other people could not tune out his father's shrieking. "One last head! One last head!"

One night, he told the bartender the whole story, and it became a joke among the townspeople. Every time someone mentioned seeing a Pottawatomie or Wyandot warrior in Tom's presence, folks would nudge one another knowingly. "Here's your chance, Tom," they would say. "Better go get him now, before your father's ghost returns!" Tom's life became one of sheer misery. He couldn't hold a job because of his drinking, and he was teased and tormented constantly by the wags in town over his father's curse.

Just when Tom thought things couldn't get any worse, he was visited at midnight by the rotting corpse of his father. Bill Quick stood in the doorway, his maggot-ridden skeleton and shredding skin clear as day in the bright moonlight. The specter held a hunting rifle in one hand and a knife in the other. Pointing the rifle at his cowering son, Bill Quick made his demand. "Ninety-nine heads line my walls! You must kill one last Indian and fulfill my oath to your grandfather!"

ONE LAST HEAD

Tom was so terrified he couldn't speak. He backed away until his shoulders hit the wall behind him. His body was shaking uncontrollably. He wanted to flee, but he stood frozen in place, unable to take his eyes off the demented figure in the doorway. "One last head!" the corpse shrieked, a piece of its lip dropping off as it howled. "I need one last head. You have until midnight, or the spirit of your murdered grandfather will return with me, and you will answer to him."

Tom's courage broke, and with it went his mind. With a shriek every bit as horrible as that of his father, he dove out the window and ran toward the settlement. His screams of terror woke the whole town. He leapt from house to house, pounding on the wooden doors until they buckled, babbling insanely about his father's specter, and begging someone, anyone, to take him in. The good people of the town barred their doors, and the townsmen ran him off with rifles, fearing that the drunken madman might harm their women and children.

Tom was last seen plunging into the woods in the direction of his father's cabin. When the townsmen went to check on him the next day, they found his house empty. Taking their rifles, they started a careful search, not sure what would happen when they found the poor, insane drunk. They followed his trail easily through the woods, but the tracks disappeared just inside the clearing where the Quick cabin stood.

The air still reeked of rotting flesh. To the right of the cabin, Bill Quick's grave lay undisturbed in the flickering afternoon light. The searchers approached the cabin reluctantly, covering their noses before they entered. The main room was empty and showed signs of long abandonment. The dirt floor showed no new tracks, but there was still the back room to check.

One man crossed to the door and pulled it open. The stench of rotten flesh bellowed out into the room. Gagging desperately, the man stepped through the door and gave a cry of terror that brought the other searchers running. They were instantly overwhelmed by the grisly sight of rotting human heads lining the shelves in the room. But it was the bulging eyes and agony-twisted face of the latest victim that held their attention. Filling the one hundredth space at the center of the back wall was the head of Tom Quick. The rest of his body was never found.

13

You Just Killed Me

I grew up hearing the stories about the hitchhiking phantom that haunted a dangerous curve on the local highway. All the kids told it at camp and at sleepover parties. According to the legend, a teenage boy picked up a girl who was walking beside the road near the dangerous bend. She was shivering with cold, so he gave her his jacket and then drove her home. It wasn't until he'd seen her to the door and driven away that he realized she still had his jacket. The next day he went to the house and rang the doorbell. An old woman answered the door and looked startled and then sad when the teenager asked after the girl. "That was my daughter, who died in a car accident twenty years ago," the old woman told him. "Her ghost tries to come home on the anniversary of her death. She's buried in the churchyard next door." The old woman took the boy to the churchyard and pointed to a worn grave marker standing near the fence. Draped over the tombstone was the teenager's jacket.

"It's just an urban legend," my friend Robert said at our lunch table a few weeks before our high school graduation. "The phantom hitchhiker is the most commonly told ghost story in America."

"It also happens to be a true story," his girlfriend said hotly. "It's that ghost that causes all those crashes on that curve. When folks see her beside the road, they swerve to avoid her and crash. That's what happened to Susan and her boyfriend last year. Everyone says so."

Silence fell over the table, and everyone glanced at me. I swallowed hard and stared at my tray. I'd had a crush on Susan ever since I started noticing girls back in middle school. I'd been green with jealousy when she started going out with a senior from another high school. She was a beautiful brunette with dark-lashed gray eyes and a sweet smile for everyone she met. Everyone loved Susan. Her death was a shock to the whole community. The police thought her boyfriend had been drunk the night of the crash, but there wasn't enough left of either of them after the car fire, so we never knew for sure.

The bell rang, and everyone hurried to his or her next class. I dragged along behind, telling myself that grown men didn't cry.

Everywhere I looked that afternoon, I saw something that reminded me of Susan. By the time the final bell rang, my mood was as black as the roiling thunderclouds overhead. Instead of driving home, I headed toward the roadside memorial the senior class had put up on the highway in memory of Susan. The wind whipped against my car as I drove, and the sky was black with roiling storm clouds. A storm was chasing my heels; I couldn't linger. I pulled off to the side of the road near Susan's memorial. It was nearly buried under masses of flowers. Susan's friends and family made sure there was always something decorating her memorial.

I shut off the engine and stepped out into the wind with a bunch of flowers in my hand. I placed them at the foot of the white cross and cried a little as lightning flashed and thunder cracked a few moments later. When raindrops started to fall, I ran hastily back to my car and flipped on the headlights. Time to go.

As the heavens opened above me and rain poured down in sheets, I drove slowly down the road toward home. I could hardly see in the heavy rain, so when a white figure darted into the road in front of me, I barely had time to slam on my brakes, praying I wouldn't hit it. As my car skidded to a halt, I gasped in amazement, recognizing Susan. I'd know that face anywhere! Susan was alive and well—not to mention soaking wet and waving for me to stop the car.

"Susan," I shouted as she pulled open the passenger door and jumped into the car. "You're alive," I said hoarsely, tears pouring down my face. Susan's face was white as a sheet, and rain dripped from her clothes and dark hair.

"Take me home. I want to go home," Susan said in a strained voice.

"Of course," I said, responding immediately to the urgency in her tone. I put on my blinker, preparing to drive toward her house. Susan grabbed my arm with an ice-cold hand and said, "Not that way. We have to go through the curve. I need to make it past the curve."

A shiver ran through my body at her words, and I glanced over at the girl seated beside me. In the dim twilight of the storm, her body glowed faintly and seemed to ripple under my gaze. My blood ran cold at the sight. Susan wasn't alive after all. She was a ghost.

"Why do you want to drive away from your house? I thought you wanted to go home," I said carefully, keeping my tone neutral and my body completely still. An odd little bubble of time seemed to surround the two of us.

"I have to make it through the curve," Susan repeated, her eyes glowing with tears. "I must make it through!"

"I think we should go home the regular way," I said.

"No!" the ghost screamed in fury. "No!"

Terrified, I turned the car around and headed slowly back toward the deadly curve in the highway. Rain pounded on the roof of the car. Lightning flashed and thunder roared, but the storm held no terror for me now. All my attention was on the glowing figure beside me.

"Drive faster," the ghost of Susan commanded. "You are going too slow. We must make it through the curve."

"I will not drive faster in this rain. It isn't safe," I said, my voice high-pitched with fear.

"Why won't you listen to me?" Susan shouted. "Give me the wheel!"

Translucent hands gripped the wheel beside mine, fighting me for control of the car.

"Let go!" I screamed, trying to wrench the wheel away from the determined ghost. "Susan, let go of the wheel!" My words came out as white puffs of steam in the frigid air. A spectral wind whipped the inside of the car. The vehicle swerved drunkenly left, right, left as the ghost and I fought over the wheel.

"You will not kill me again!" the phantom woman screamed in my ear. "Never again!"

"Let go of the wheel," I roared, jerking it violently away her. My hands passed right through the white translucent arms and

YOU JUST KILLED ME

torso of the ghost. The car hydroplaned and started spinning out of control as we reached the deadly curve.

"Nooooooo!" the phantom and I screamed together as the car smashed through the fence and flipped over twice. I felt my neck crack as my head smashed against the headrest. White-hot pain roared through my body. The airbag exploded into my face.

As the world went black, I heard Susan's ghost sobbing, "You just killed me!"

My final thought was, "So did you."

14

The Scorned Suitor

WAYNE COUNTY

Marie was frustrated with her handsome suitor. Canadian Lieutenant William Muir had called on her every week for nearly a year but had been too shy to declare himself. Marie was irritated by the delay. Was he ever going to propose? She loved William, but he was driving her crazy. Marie tried to hurry him up, but she had already dropped more hints than were considered proper for a well-bred young female. And he wasn't taking the hint! Her friends all teased her about her shy suitor, and their comments were not always kind. The other girls thought something must be wrong with Marie, since she couldn't get a simple marriage proposal out of her man.

Finally, in August 1812, on the eve of his first battle in the British war against the Americans, William came to ask for Marie's hand in marriage. Like all the other soldiers, he wanted to get things settled with his sweetheart before facing possible death. William's dark eyes flashed with love as he knelt before Marie in the lovely garden, pouring out his heart.

William's proposal was everything Marie had longed for all those months he had come calling each week and never spoken his heart. But a small part of her—the not very nice part—

wished to revenge itself on her suitor for all those weeks of frustrated waiting. It was fashionable in those days to dally with a man before accepting his proposal, so instead of accepting the lieutenant—as she fully intended to do—Marie rolled her eyes and trilled coquettishly: "La, William, you cannot be serious. Why should I marry you?"

It was a mistake. Marie held her breath, hoping to hear further protestations of love from this handsome man wearing the crisp red uniform of a British lieutenant. Instead, William pulled back in hurt and shock as though Marie had slapped him. All the color drained from his face.

"I am sorry to have disturbed you with my unwelcome feelings," William said stiffly, rising to his feet. "I bid you farewell."

Marie's mouth fell open in surprise. Before she could assemble a thought, William spun on his heel and marched down the garden path toward the front of the house. Marie stared after him in disbelief. Then fear flooded through her. Had she lost her suitor forever with her coquettish answer?

Marie sprang from the garden seat and rushed after him, crying, "Wait, William, wait! I did not mean it. I was teasing you." She rounded the corner just in time to see William's horse trotting away down the long driveway. His red uniform gleaming in the setting sun, the handsome Canadian lieutenant vanished in a cloud of dust, never once looking back.

"What have I done?" Marie wailed, dread clutching at her heart. Her William was going away that very hour to lead a British raid against an American settlement across the Detroit River. What if he never came back? She covered her face with her hands and stood shaking with fear and despair for a very long time.

It took Marie hours to fall asleep that night. Every time she closed her eyes, she saw the hurt look on William's face and she writhed with guilt. Finally, sleep put her out of her misery, if only for a very short time.

In the middle of the night, Marie snapped awake from a restless, despair-ridden sleep, sure that she heard footsteps coming into her room. She sat up, clutching the bedspread to her chest and then gasped with surprise. Standing a foot away was the tall figure of Lieutenant William Muir; his shape outlined by the flickering firelight.

"William, what are you doing in my bedroom? It is not proper," she whispered hoarsely. Then her sleep-filled eyes widened as she realized there was no fire burning in the grate on this warm August night. It was William himself who was glowing. His body was stiff and lifeless. As he turned to face her properly, she saw a gaping red hole in the center of his forehead.

"Oh dear God," she cried, realizing that she was seeing a ghost.

"Do not be afraid, Marie," William's spirit said in a hollow voice. "I fell in battle with the Americans this evening, and my body lies unseen in a thicket. I beg you to rescue me from the beasts of the forest before my body is despoiled."

"William, oh William, I am sorry," Marie gasped. "I shouldn't have refused you. I didn't mean it. Please forgive me!"

William's ghost continued as if she had not spoken: "My death was not in vain. The Americans will not triumph for long. Soon the flag of England will fly over Detroit."

For a moment, the dead man's eyes stared deeply into hers and Marie saw a flood of images: happy dreams of what might have been between them had William lived, the terror of the battlefield, and finally the path that led to the place where William's body lay hidden in the bushes. The images ceased abruptly, leaving Marie dazed and shaking with fear and remorse.

"Fare you well, Marie. May you be happy," William intoned in the hollow voice of the dead. The glowing figure in the blood-red uniform reached out and grasped Marie by the hand, squeezing it in a tight clasp. His hand was so cold it blackened Marie's flesh like frostbite. Marie screamed in fear and pain. Then she fainted.

When Marie regained consciousness, the ghost was gone, but the mark of his ghostly clasp was still burned onto her hand. She stared at the mark in the lantern light, knowing she must do something about the ghost's message. She had to atone for her unthinking cruelty to her lost suitor.

Rising, Marie dressed with difficulty, for her damaged hand would barely function. She went to the stables and saddled a horse. She rode to the British camp and awakened the old Wyandot war chief who was a dear family friend. Marie told him the whole sad story and begged him to help her find William's body.

The old chief and a few of his men pushed their canoes into the water and escorted the trembling girl across the Detroit River. As soon as she set foot on the night-darkened shore, Marie could see the way she should go as plainly as if it was marked on a map. Though he was not visible, Marie knew William's ghost was helping her. She led the warriors directly to the place William had imprinted on her mind.

THE SCORNED SUITOR

The Wyandot pushed their way into the thicket and found William's body right where the ghost said it would be. William lay on his side, a gaping red bullet hole in the middle of his forehead. They carried the body gravely to the waiting canoes and brought the dead lieutenant back to his camp in Canada. In the morning, William was properly laid to rest, as befit a hero who gave his life for his country. Marie stood by his grave and cried disconsolately for the lover she had scorned.

The spirit's burn mark never faded from Marie's hand. Neither did her feeling of guilt. She aged overnight and spent the rest of her life trying to atone for her cruelty to her handsome lieutenant. As for William, his ghost can still be seen marching through the woods on the anniversary of the Battle of Monguagon, saber in hand and a gaping red hole in his forehead.

15

The Telephone Call

GRAND RAPIDS

When I went to work for Bell Telephone all those years ago, I had no idea that my new job would involve a ghost. It certainly wasn't part of the job description, or you can be sure I would never have interviewed for the position. I was fresh out of school and aching to prove myself in the grown-up world of business, so I didn't pay any attention to the rumors around town that said that Bell Telephone might not be the smartest place to work.

On my first day of work, my supervisor escorted me to the second floor of the building to show me the desk they had assigned me and help me settle in. As soon as the elevator doors opened on the second-floor hallway, I felt a rush of cold air wash over me and my heart started thumping faster. This was not a good place; I knew it immediately. Goose bumps raised on my arms and the back of my neck. I wanted to push the down button on the elevator, but my supervisor stepped into the hallway, chatting amiably about my duties as though nothing was wrong. I forced myself to follow. My desk was in the far corner of the floor, which did not feel as cold, although the goose bumps remained on my neck. However, the challenge of first-day tasks soon drove away my sense of danger, and I absorbed myself in learning the ropes.

That night when I got home, I had the first dream. A woman was frantically running down the long second-floor hallway of the Bell Telephone building. A sense of menace shadowed her, and she wanted desperately to get away before it was too late. Her fear was so strong that I awoke sweating in panic, a scream on my lips. My legs were trembling as though I'd tried to run in my sleep. I turned on the light with shaking fingers, panting with fear. When my breathing calmed a bit, I went to get some water to wash away the taste of the dream.

Golly Moses, but I didn't want to go back to work in the morning. Not after a dream like that. But I was poor and had bills to pay. It was a good job that would further my ambitious career plans, so off I went, in spite of my reservations. I braced myself for the rush of fear and cold air that poured into the elevator when the doors opened on the haunted hallway and hurried to my desk as fast as I could.

The second day was much better than the first. I was getting to know my colleagues and had more work to do. I could ignore the spooky feeling around me.

Wishing to avoid the hallway leading to the elevator, I took the stairs when I went out to get lunch. This was a mistake. The stairs were dark and narrow and seemed even more menacing than the second-floor hallway. I almost turned back and then told myself it was just one flight of stairs. What could happen? As soon as my foot hit the first step, the dark threatening presence I had felt in my dream surrounded me. My breath was abruptly cut off as though cold hands had clamped themselves around my throat. Choking, I raced toward the bottom and burst out

THE TELEPHONE CALL

onto the first floor, praying for salvation. I fled through the front door and out into the street. Immediately, the presence vanished. I found myself leaning against the next building over, panting for breath as curious passersby stared at my white face and shaking body.

The whole encounter was over within moments, but my legs shook for nearly an hour afterward. No wonder my supervisor always took the long walk down the hallway to the elevator, even though her desk was right below mine. I would never go down that staircase again!

I'd like to say things got better, but that would be a lie. I enjoyed the work. I enjoyed my supervisor. I enjoyed my colleagues. But I hated the building more and more each day. And every night I dreamed of the fleeing woman with the frantic eyes. Sometimes I heard a funny *thump-thud* sound behind her, like uneven footsteps. It made the dream even worse, for the sound was somehow associated with the dark presence that had tried to strangle me on the staircase. By the end of my second week, I had dark circles under my eyes that no makeup could hide, and I jumped whenever someone spoke to me.

On Monday of my third week, I smelled something funny when I got to my desk. It was a rotten smell—decaying flesh mixed with the acrid stench of gas. It made me choke. For a moment I almost threw up. Then the smell was gone. I fell into my chair, shaking all over.

The woman who sat next to me rushed over to see what was wrong. Terrified, I gasped out the whole story, starting with the cold and fear I felt when I first stepped onto the second floor and ending with the terrible dreams and the stench of rotting flesh mixed with gas. The woman stared wide-eyed as I whispered my tale through tight lips.

"No one told you about this place?" she asked when I finished my tale.

"Told me what?" I asked, rubbing my eyes with trembling hands.

"About the murder," my colleague whispered, her eyes darting around to make sure our supervisor was not present. Then she told me the story as I sat with my head bowed and my hand over my mouth to keep from vomiting.

A young Detroit couple moved to Grand Rapids back in 1907 when the husband got a job working as a brakeman with the Grand Rapids and Indiana Railroad. The couple seemed quite happy in their new home, until a horrific accident on the railroad took the young husband's leg and he was fitted with a wooden peg instead. Though he was physically healed, the husband's mind was soured and twisted by the accident. Angry and brooding, he began accusing his wife of infidelity. The couple's shouted arguments could be heard all over the neighborhood, and one night the husband was observed chasing his wife down the street with a straight razor in his hand. Soon afterward, the wife left him.

Things in the neighborhood got quiet for a week or two. Then the husband contacted the wife to say he wanted her back. She agreed to meet with him, and the neighbors saw them driving together in their carriage, talking soberly to each other. They parked the vehicle and together went into their old home to continue talking. This was the last anyone saw of them, and some folks thought the estranged couple had reconciled and left the city.

Then the neighbors began complaining about a ghastly smell coming from the abandoned house. The authorities were called to investigate. When the police broke into the house, they were overwhelmed by the stench of rotting flesh and leaking gas. They found the bodies of the husband and wife in the bedroom. The wife had been bludgeoned to death by her husband's wooden leg before he committed suicide by unscrewing a gas fixture on the wall and slitting his own throat.

"Afterward, the house was so haunted that they had to tear it down," my colleague whispered fearfully. "The lot remained vacant until this building was built in its place."

As the woman's story progressed, I became more and more aware of the smell of gas permeating the room. The dark presence was all around us, listening to her tale. It was getting harder and harder for me to breath. By the time she finished her story, sweat was pouring down my face and I was panting for breath. She clutched my hands, ready to call for an ambulance, but I shook her off and grabbed my handbag.

"I need to get out of here," I told her. "I'm going home."

"Do you want me to walk you to the elevator?" she asked.

"No!" I said quickly. "Thank you. I will be fine."

As soon as I stepped into the hall, I regretted my refusal. A rotten stench swelled around me, and the fear pulsing through the frigid air made my hair stand on end. In a terrible parody of my nightmare, I rushed frantically toward the elevator, aware of a *thump-thud* sound behind me—the noise a man with a wooden leg would make. For a moment, it was as though the woman in my dream and I had become the same person. Burning bile rose in my throat and tainted my mouth. Death was so close I could almost feel the first stunning blow.

As I reached the elevator, it chimed and the door opened, revealing my supervisor. I flung myself into the elevator as she exited, shouting, "I quit! You should have told me this place was haunted!"

The door slid shut on her stupefied expression. As the elevator plunged toward the first floor, the smell and the sense of cold and fear faded. I hurried into a nearby ladies room and lost my breakfast in the toilet. Then I made my way back to my apartment as best I could in my terrified state. I bought several newspapers on my way past a corner newsstand. I needed to find another job.

As I was combing the want ads just before bed that night, the phone rang. I rather thought the caller would be my former supervisor, who owed me an apology for the dangerous situation into which she'd thrust me. But the voice on the other end of the line was breathless and other-worldly. I knew at once it was the voice of the woman in my dream. It gasped, "Help me. *Help me*. He's coming!" Through the receiver, I heard a menacing *thump-thud, thump-thud*. The woman screamed deafeningly into my right ear and the phone went dead.

I screamed too. I couldn't help it. It was too much. First the ghost haunted my dreams, and now she was calling me on the telephone? I rushed to my bedroom and started packing my bags. I was not going to stay in this haunted city for another night.

My parents took care of vacating my Grand Rapids apartment while I stayed in Ann Arbor with my sister to recover from my traumatic experience. While I was there, I found a good job and a wonderful new life, blessedly free of ghosts. But I still don't like answering the telephone.

16

Don't Sell My House

CENTRAL MICHIGAN

When Tilly's daughter, Lisa, married a nice widower after an extremely short courtship, the newlyweds bought a beautiful new RV and had it installed on their property so Tilly could have a place of her own to live. It was a nice arrangement for her. She had her privacy, but she was close enough to walk to her daughter's house whenever she chose—which was often, because she and Lisa were very close.

Mark had built the house for his first wife, who had died of cancer two years before his marriage to Lisa. It was a small, two-story cottage with a finished basement. Tilly had her own key to the basement door so she could do her laundry whenever she pleased without disturbing her daughter and son-in-law.

About a year after Lisa and Mark's wedding, they found out that they were expecting twins. Tilly was delighted with the news that she was going to be a grandmother, but she was concerned that the house was rather small for a double addition to the family. After talking it over, Mark and Lisa put the cottage up for sale and started searching for a bigger house with enough property to house Tilly's RV. And that's when the problems began.

Tilly noticed it first. Suddenly, the cottage was filled from night until morning with the distinctive smell of expensive perfume. Lisa was allergic to perfume and never wore it, so the source of the smell was a mystery. The first time Mark smelled it, he turned pale and grimly told Tilly that it was the scent his dead wife had favored.

Then furniture that Lisa had rearranged when she first came to the little cottage abruptly moved back to its original place. Tilly knocked her shins several times on a side table that would not stay put. Dishes moved from one cupboard to another, the sofa was pushed back against the wall, and the books in Mark's study were taken out of their categories and put in alphabetical order, the way his former wife had kept them arranged. Tilly was sure that the ghost of Mark's first wife had returned to the little cottage. But why? If she was jealous of Lisa, why had it taken her a whole year to manifest herself?

One afternoon, Tilly was down in the basement doing her laundry while Mark and Lisa were out discussing the sale of the cottage with their attorney. They had just received a generous bid on the house and had decided to accept it. Tilly was emptying the washing machine when she became aware of movement by the staircase leading to the kitchen. Tilly turned and saw a young woman floating a foot above the staircase, wearing a white dress sprinkled with pink flowers. Tilly froze in shock, the laundry basket shaking in her hands.

"Don't sell my house," the young woman said.

Tilly swallowed convulsively, not sure what she should say or do.

"This is my house. Don't sell my house!" the woman said again. Her pretty face was suddenly transformed with rage, and she shook her fist at Tilly. Tilly gave a shriek of fear, dropped the basket of wet laundry, and ran for the outside door. Hands shaking, she yanked it open and raced across the lawn toward her RV.

Slamming the trailer door behind her, Tilly locked it and sank down into a chair, gasping for breath. All at once, the RV started shaking violently, as if someone were pushing against it.

"Don't sell my house!" a voice wailed outside. "Don't sell my house!" Fists began pounding against the door so violently that the metal dented. Tilly fled to the back of the RV and locked herself in the bathroom.

"Don't sell my house," the phantom exclaimed again, shaking the RV until Tilly was sure it would tip over. "If you sell my house, something terrible will happen to your family! Don't sell my house!"

The roar of a car engine pierced the ghost's words. Abruptly, the shaking and pounding ceased. A moment later, Mark and Lisa's car pulled into the driveway. A hysterical Tilly ran out to meet them and told them the whole story.

Mark was upset. As soon as Tilly described the ghost, he recognized her as his dead wife. Until that moment, he had forgotten that he promised his first wife that he would never sell the cottage. But what else could they do? Mark and Lisa needed a bigger house for their growing family, and they could not afford to buy one without selling the cottage.

Mark and Lisa called in their priest to try to appease the spirit of Mark's first wife. The holy man prayed over the cottage and pleaded at length with the photo of the phantom, begging her to release Mark from his promise. The only response he received was the choking smell of expensive perfume, which

DON'T SELL MY HOUSE

became so overwhelming that he was forced to leave the cottage until it dissipated.

After much discussion, Mark and Lisa decided to defy the phantom and sell the cottage. Everyone was anxious up to the day of the closing, but nothing further happened. There was no smell of perfume, no rearranging of the furniture, no ectoplasmic appearances. They concluded that the ghost must have listened to the priest and decided to leave them in peace. But Tilly was still nervous. She was the only one to have seen the phantom, and the ghost had not struck Tilly as someone willing to give up easily.

On the night following the family's move from the cottage, Lisa was struck with a terrible pain in her abdomen. Mark rushed her to the hospital, where she gave birth prematurely to the twins, who were stillborn. On his way home from the hospital, Mark's car was struck by a truck, and he was killed instantly. At the same moment, Lisa sat bolt upright in her hospital bed, staring at an empty corner of the room. She screamed once in terror at the sight of the phantom floating before her eyes, and flung up her arms to ward off the specter. Then her eyes rolled back in her head and she fell back on the pillows, dead instantly from a brain aneurism.

Of the three people living on the property when the ghost appeared, Tilly was the only one who survived the ghost's curse. But the overwhelming grief caused by the loss of her family broke her spirit and turned her mind. Within a week after leaving the cottage, Tilly was admitted to an insane asylum, where she spent the rest of her days weeping bitterly and begging her dead daughter not to sell their house.

17

The Ghost's Cap

ANN ARBOR

A full moon hung in the star-speckled sky as Anya climbed out her second-story bedroom window into the cold autumn night and shimmied down the bare oak tree. The chilly air didn't bother her. She was on her way to the graveyard to win a bet against the supercilious Ivan and his annoying little sister. The prosperous children of a local farmer, Ivan and his sister often took pleasure in teasing Anya about her worn clothing and old boots. But this time the joke was on them. Ivan had bet the fancy silver buttons from his best coat and a yard of handmade lace from his sister's petticoat if Anya could learn the name of the ghost that sat on a tombstone in the local cemetery from midnight until dawn each night. Because Anya didn't believe in ghosts, she was going to invent some nonsense to tell the gullible Ivan and his sister. But first she must walk to the graveyard past Ivan's house; she knew they wouldn't believe her story unless they witnessed her nighttime journey firsthand.

A wild wind shook the treetops as Anya stalked past Ivan's house. She made certain her face was clearly visible under the streetlamp, knowing that Ivan and his sister were watching from the window to see if she was brave enough to take them up on their bet.

At the gate to the cemetery, Anya paused uncertainly, seeing a white figure seated on a gravestone partway down one narrow aisle. The wind moaned around her, and she clutched her shawl close, shivering in the cold air. Then she realized the white figure must be Ivan, trying to trick her into believing there really was a ghost in the cemetery. Really, that boy! It was time someone taught him a lesson.

Anya pulled open the gate and stalked down the narrow passage between the gravestones until she stood in front of the white figure. Ivan had obviously taken some trouble with his disguise. The old man seated on the gravestone had his hands folded in his lap, and his white clothes glowed in the moonlight. His wrinkled skin was corpse gray, there were dark rings under his cavernous dark eyes, and he wore a white cap just like the one Ivan had described. That cap annoyed Anya. Whoever heard of a ghost wearing a cap? She reached out and pulled the moldering covering off the white figure's head, crying, "You don't frighten me. You are not a corpse! You are a saucy boy who just lost all his silver buttons to me!" With that, she danced away between the tombs, waving the moldy white cap triumphantly above her head.

When Anya got home, she tucked the cap under her arm, nose wrinkling from the musty smell of decay, and climbed back up the tree to her window. She threw the moldering white cap through the window into the darkest corner of her room and slid in after it. Closing the window against the cold air, Anya slipped into her nightdress and went to bed. She didn't hear the wind pick up shortly after she fell asleep, nor did she see a white figure floating outside the window, peering in at the glowing white cap in the corner of the room. "Give me back my cap," the figure called, tapping the glass with a shimmering finger. "Give me back my cap."

Anya turned over in bed and covered her head with the pillow, ignoring the tapping sound at the window. "It's just the branches of the oak tree," she told herself sleepily.

"Give me back my cap," the figure called again. It rattled the window with a decaying hand as Anya snuggled deeper into the covers. "Give me back my cap!" The wind gusted against the house, shaking it from top to bottom. But Anya slept on.

"My cap!" howled the floating ghost. Its cry was taken up by the autumn wind and blown all over the village, making dogs howl and cats yowl and the good farm folk shiver in their beds. But Anya did not stir. She knew there was no such thing as ghosts.

Dawn came and the glowing figure vanished with a frustrated pop. In the dusty corner of Anya's bedroom, the ghostly light faded from the white cap.

After breakfast, Anya went to Ivan's house to collect her bet. "I went to the graveyard," she said, "and I met the ghost of Old Peter. He gave me this hat as proof!" She waved the cap in the faces of Ivan and his sister. Ivan stared glumly at the decrepit white cap, which was filled with grave dust and mold. Sadly, he cut the silver buttons from his fine coat, and his sister removed the expensive lace from her petticoat. They gave their prized items to Anya, who danced triumphantly away with the buttons and lace in her pocket and the foul white cap on top of her yellow curls.

On her way home, Anya grabbed the smelly cap from her head and threw it into the river. "Good riddance to bad rubbish," she called as it sank beneath an eddy. "Honestly. Whoever heard of a ghost wearing a cap?"

That night Anya stayed up late sewing silver buttons on her coat and trimming her petticoat with lace. Then she bade her parents a cheerful good night and went to bed. Just before dawn, the wind howled and slammed into the old house, rattling every window and shaking every door. "Give me back my cap!" a white figure roared, hovering beside the oak tree. "Give me back my cap!" But Anya slept on, dreaming of her new silver buttons and lace.

In the next bedroom, her parents woke in fear, hearing the ghostly voice howling like thunder just outside their house. "Give me back my cap," the floating figure shouted in rage. The wind slammed the shutters again and again. The air in the bedroom grew so cold it burned the nostrils and made the parents' breath crystallize into a fog around their heads. The figure hovering outside glowed with an eerie blue-white light that illuminated every corner of their room.

"What is that thing?" screamed the mother, hiding beneath the covers. Trembling from head to foot, the father stumbled to the window and shouted, "In the name of God, tell us what you want!"

"I want the cap your daughter stole," cried the ghost, his eyes blazing silver fire. Tiny lightning bolts raced up and down his white garments. Anya's parents cowered away from the terrible figure floating in wrath outside their window. Then the first ray of dawn crowned the hill behind the house, and the spirit vanished.

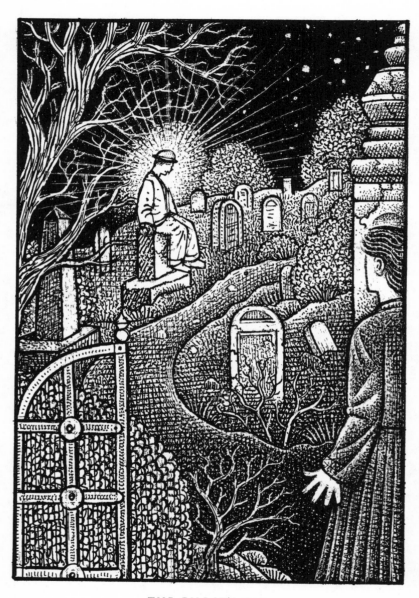

THE GHOST'S CAP

Anya's father raced to the room next door and dragged his daughter out of bed. "Where is the cap you stole from the ghost?" he shouted.

Anya stared at him sleepily. "What do you mean, Father?" she asked. "What ghost?"

"The ghost outside our window," cried Anya's mother from the doorway.

"That's not a ghost, that's Ivan," Anya said with a yawn. "He's playing tricks again."

"Even that trickster Ivan cannot float ten feet above the ground," her father said. "Now tell me where you put that cap!"

"I threw it in the river," Anya said. "Honestly, what a fuss!"

"Threw it in the river. Ah me! The ghost will destroy us when it finds out," cried the mother, wringing her hands. "Father, you must go for the priest."

The mother scolded Anya soundly while the father fetched the local priest and explained the situation to him. The priest stared gravely at the erring Anya, who glared back, annoyed by this unnecessary fuss.

"You must come to the church now, and we will ring the bell for Mass so the good citizens can pray for your soul," the priest said. "If enough of us pray, the ghost may leave you alone."

"What nonsense," grumbled Anya as her parents dragged her to the church. The priest rang the bell, and the local residents came to pray. The priest made Anya kneel in front of the altar while he read a prayer for the dead. Behind her, the good people of the town listened gravely, staring at the defiant girl who dared deface the dead.

All at once a massive whirlwind blew in from the south. Black clouds darkened over the sky, the trees bent double in the blast, and then the church was shaken by a blow like that of a giant's hand. The doors blew open and the whirlwind howled inside, tossing hymnals and Bibles and candles and icons to the floor. The walls shook, the stained-glass windows shattered, and the congregation fell to the floor. At the altar, Anya gave a bloodcurdling scream as the lights went out.

All at once the roaring wind and the earthquake stopped. A loosened portrait thudded to the floor in the silence, and a candle toppled from its holder and rolled to the foot of the altar. The eyes of every person in the room followed the candle as it stopped at the empty railing where, moments before, Anya had knelt in a defiant rage. There was nothing there now save a few long golden curls, a handful of silver buttons, and a bit of lace.

PART TWO

Powers of Darkness and Light

18

Windigo

ISLE ROYALE NATIONAL PARK

His wife was so ill during the autumn that they could not move south with the tribe, lest the journey kill her. So the little family stayed on the island for the winter, gathering as much wood and food as they could to stave off the cold and the dark demons the snow brought with it.

They were comfortable enough at first. Under the care of her mother-in-law and husband, the wife began to regain her strength. But as the winter grew fiercer, the enforced captivity and the slowly dwindling food stores lowered the family's spirits, and the wife's newly gained strength drained away.

Finally, there came a mighty blizzard that lasted so long they thought they would perish. After many days the wind and swirling snow died away, and the husband ventured outside. The next storm was already on the horizon, but if food was not found soon, the family would starve. With the memory of his poor wife's thin face and weak form ever before his eyes, the warrior set forth into the white, featureless landscape to check his traps and to hunt for game.

Keeping his knife and spear close, he ventured out upon the most frequently used game trail, watching intently for animal tracks in the newly fallen snow. He saw none, but he stayed alert, watching for movement of any kind, however small. The forest lay still and oddly silent under its gleaming coating of ice and snow as he checked each of his traps. All were empty. Every creature with a shred of sense lay deep within its burrow, sleeping through the terrible winter storms. Still, the warrior hunted, knowing how desperate his family had become.

As he moved through the eerie stillness, broken only by the soft whisper of the wind blowing from the lake, the warrior heard a strange hissing. It seemed to come from everywhere and nowhere at once. He stopped, his heart pounding. Then he saw blood-soaked footprints appearing on the path in front of him, coming straight toward him. He swallowed convulsively and gripped his knife more tightly, knowing that somewhere, watching him, was a Windigo.

He had learned about the Windigo at his father's knee. It was a large creature, as tall as a tree, with a lipless mouth and jagged teeth. Its breath was a strange hiss, its footprints full of blood, and it ate any man, woman, or child who ventured into its territory. The poor murder victims were considered the lucky ones. Sometimes, the Windigo chose to possess a person instead, and then the luckless individual became a Windigo himself, hunting down those he had once loved and feasting upon their flesh.

The warrior knew he would have just one chance to prevail over the Windigo. After that, he would die. Or . . . he shied away from the thought, too terrible to contemplate.

Cautiously, the warrior backed away from the bloody footprints. The red tracks halted abruptly a few feet from him, leaving him with no inkling of where the Windigo might be hiding, or from where it might attack. He kept listening to the hissing breath of the monster. Was it stronger in one direction?

Gripping his spear tightly in one hand, his knife in the other, the warrior tried in vain to look everywhere at once. Then the snowbank to his left erupted in an icy spray as the creature leapt out at him. The warrior dove to one side, rolling in the snow so that his clothing was covered with the white powder and he became harder to see in the gray twilight of the approaching storm.

The Windigo whirled its massive frame as the warrior threw his spear. It struck the creature's chest, but the Windigo shook it off as if it were a toy. The warrior crouched behind a small tree as the creature searched for him. His half-starved body shook with fear. He gripped his knife hard, afraid it would fall from his trembling hand. The warrior knew that he had strength in his famished body for only one more encounter with the monster. If he did not prevail then, he was doomed, and his family with him.

The Windigo loomed over his hiding place, its sharp eyes spotting his outline against the tree. It bent down, long arms reaching. The warrior leapt forward as if to embrace the creature and thrust his knife up into one enormous black eye. The Windigo howled in pain as the blade of the knife sliced into its brain cavity. It tried to pull the warrior off of its chest with its sharp claws, but the warrior clung to the creature, stabbing it again and again in the eyes, in the head.

Slowly the Windigo collapsed to the ground, bleeding profusely, almost crushing the warrior beneath its bulk. The warrior pulled himself loose and stared at the creature, which blended in with its white surroundings so well that he would

WINDIGO

not have seen it save for the blood pouring from its eyes and ears and scalp. The outline of the creature grew misty and then vanished completely, leaving only a pool of blood to indicate where it had fallen.

Shaken, his heart pounding with fear and fatigue, the warrior picked himself up, cleaned his knife with shaking hands, recovered his spear, and turned for home. There was no time left to seek for game. The new storm would break at any moment, and he would die if he did not seek shelter. He prayed that what little food they had left would carry them through this next blizzard, though he knew in his heart it could not.

At the edge of the wood, he found himself face to face with a red fox. It was a fat old creature, its muzzle lined with gray. The animal stood very still and gazed at him with wise, tired old eyes. The warrior's heart leapt with hope. Here was the food his family needed to survive until spring; brought to him like a gift from the spirits as a reward for killing the evil Windigo. With a prayer of thanksgiving, the warrior killed the fox and took it home to his starving family. The meat lasted for many days until the final storm had blown itself out and the warrior could hunt safely once more.

19

Paul Bunyan and the Witch

CHEBOYGAN

It was springtime in the north woods. The sun was warming up the world, the snowbanks were shrinking, and the birds were coming back to sing their hearts out and do some romancing. But the lumberjacks in the camp were all a little blue, in spite of the hustle and bustle in the woods around them. Paul Bunyan and Babe had left the camp on the first day of spring to scout out some new timberland for lumbering, and things were mighty dull without them. The men had to leave the trees piled on the ground until Babe could haul them out to the lake, and it took them all day long to cut a stand of trees that Paul Bunyan could have cut down in an hour.

Even the cook—Sourdough Sam—missed the great lumberjack. Sam had to work night and day to keep the camp fed when Paul was home, but now he let his acre-long stove—the one that was taller than a scrub pine and could melt the snow for 20 miles around it—go out. Compared with feeding the massive lumberjack, it was a piece of cake to feed the rest of the men. Sam could whip up a meal for everyone in the whole camp using his little stove and still have time to wash dishes and write some poetry in between meals. Yes, Sam had too much time on his hands, and that's how all the trouble got started.

Sourdough Sam took to wandering through the woods during his free hours, and one afternoon, he floated into camp with a beatific look on his face and a sparkle in his eye. While the lumberjacks watched in shock, Sam cracked open the ice on the river and took a bath, right before their very eyes. And it wasn't even June!

"What's he doing that fer, Johnny?" the blacksmith asked Johnny Inkslinger, who did all the accounts for Paul Bunyan and was considered a brain by the other lumberjacks.

"I ain't too sure, Olaf," said Johnny, "but it looks to me like Sam might be in love."

The lumberjacks snickered. Sourdough Sam in love? With whom? There weren't any dames out here in the backwoods of Michigan.

But now Sam was dressing in his best clothes and combing his beard and digging under the snow, trying to find some early blooming flowers. And he was humming a funny sort of tune, the kind the ladies all liked to hear. The lumberjacks were amazed, and they nudged at Johnny Inkslinger until he went up to the cook and asked him what was what. Sam's whole face lit up, and he started talking a mile a minute and gesturing with his hands. Once he broke out into a song and a dance. Then he picked up some snowdrops that he'd found beside the bunkhouse where the snow had melted and made his way out of camp.

The men all clustered around Johnny Inkslinger. "What did he say?" they demanded.

"He's in love alright," said Johnny. "He met up with a widow woman who was setting up shop in a cottage near the river. She's a witch by trade, and she's going to make her living selling herbs and spells to everyone in the north woods."

"Looks like she set a love-spell on ol' Sourdough," sniggered Olaf. And the lumberjacks all agreed.

From that moment on, things were pretty grim around the lumber camp. The men had to eat cold baked beans and stale bread, 'cause all the livelong day, Sourdough Sam was over at the widow woman's house strumming on his banjo and making up love songs. This situation went on for about two weeks. Then suddenly, Sam appeared back in camp, the stove was fired up, and there were hot flapjacks for breakfast.

"What happened to your lady friend?" Johnny asked Sourdough Sam, as the lumberjacks wolfed down bacon and pancakes.

"She couldn't cook a dad-gum lick!" Sam said in disgust. "She invited me in for dinner, and it turns out the only thing she knows how to cook is possum stew. It was the worst thing I ever ate! I knew right then she weren't the gal for me, and I told her so to her face. She was plenty mad, let me tell you! But a man's gotta do what a man's gotta do."

"I ain't too sure about that," said Johnny Inkslinger dubiously. "Maybe you should have let her down easy-like."

"Nope. Better to get it over and done with right away," said Sam, and he turned back to his flapjack flopping.

Johnny shook his head. It seemed to him that a gentleman should treat a lady a little better than that—especially if she was a witch.

But things seemed to return to normal around the lumber camp. At least, until noontime, when a whole mess of black clouds filled the sky, and the wind started whipping the trees so hard they nearly bent double, and a whole host of eerie voices screamed from the sky: "Sourdough Sam! Sourdough Sam!"

The lumberjacks came running into camp from every part of the woods, and they all huddled under their blankets in the bunkhouse as the windstorm raged for hours above them.

"I think that widder-woman is mad at you, Sam," said Olaf.

"You oughtn't to have jilted her," said Dutch Jack, the best logger in camp when Paul Bunyan was away. And the other men agreed. Sourdough Sam didn't say anything; he just cowered beneath his blanket while dark figures swirled through the camp, shrieking his name.

Along about sunset, the lumberjacks heard a familiar voice booming over the screeching wraiths and howling wind.

"What in tarnation is going on here?" shouted Paul Bunyan.

Beside him, Babe the Blue Ox bellowed so loudly he knocked over a dozen trees. The men gave a cheer and raced outside the bunkhouse in time to see Paul bundling up a bunch of gray-hooded creatures and tossing them clean over the hill. Babe was swishing his tail so hard that it set up a counter-wind that blew the dark clouds away. Within five minutes, the camp was cleared of all the phantoms, and the last rays of the sun were beaming down through the trees.

"Now somebody had better explain what's going on," Paul Bunyan said mildly, fingering his double-bladed axe. He looked at Johnny Inkslinger, who gulped and started forward. But he was stopped by Sourdough Sam, who pushed his way to the front of the crowd. "I reckon this is my fault," Sam said.

Babe the Blue Ox leaned down and snorted in his face, nearly knocking Sam over in search of a snack. Sam thumped the great beast on the nose affectionately, swallowed a few times, and told Paul Bunyan the whole story.

"Well," said Paul when Sourdough Sam had stuttered to a close. "I don't blame the lady for being a bit testy over the way you jilted her. But she may have worked out her temper by now."

"I hope so," said Sam fervently. Johnny Inkslinger just shook his head. He was the best educated of the lot, and he remembered his mama telling him that hell had no fury like a woman scorned. And if ever there was a woman scorned, it was that witch-woman of Sam's.

Paul Bunyan said no more about it, and soon the camp had resumed its normal nightly routine. The late shift went on duty, and Sam whipped up a nice dinner to welcome the massive lumberjack home.

But the witch woman wasn't through with Sourdough Sam, and her next curse caught up with him in the morning. When Sam tried to light his acre-long stove to make Paul Bunyan some flapjacks, the fire refused to burn. Each time Sam approached the griddle, the fire went out. The men had to eat cold baked beans once again for breakfast, and it made them mighty cross.

Then Sam put some bread dough up to rise, and the whole batch flopped over and melted away before his eyes. "Dad-blame it!" he shouted, and mixed up another batch. This one floated away as fast as the first had disappeared.

Around midday, there came a chorus of growls, and a whole mess of grizzly bears overran the camp, coughing out Sourdough Sam's name. All the men shimmied up into the trees as fast as they could climb and gave a shout for Paul Bunyan, who was logging nearby. Well, as soon as those bears saw the giant lumberjack, they turned tail and ran. Paul Bunyan was pretty cross by then, what with the cold breakfast and having to leave his work to rescue a few lily-livered fellows who were scared of some little grizzly bears.

With a thunderous frown, he turned to go back into the woods, but stopped when he heard a terrible roaring coming from the lake. A massive shower of water came plummeting from the sky, and Babe could be heard grunting and stomping and bellowing with all his might. Paul Bunyan ran toward the lake, followed by all the lumberjacks in camp. They found Babe standing with all four feet planted on the bank of the lake with a gigantic sea serpent the size of New Jersey attached to the end of his nose. The serpent was trying to pull Babe into the lake, and Babe was trying to pull the serpent onto the land. The two massive creatures were churning up the lake so bad that it was creating tidal waves in Canada.

"This is the last straw!" shouted Paul Bunyan. Stalking over to the lake, he grabbed hold of the sea serpent behind its massive head and pried it off the end of Babe's nose. The serpent thrashed and struggled, but Paul just rolled it up and tied it into a knot. Then he broke off a giant pine tree at the base, hefted it onto his shoulder like a baseball bat, tossed the serpent up into the air, and batted it all the way across the country into the Pacific Ocean. The poor creature sank right to the bottom of the sea and spent a week unknotting itself. After that it minded its own business and never went near the shore again.

Once the sea serpent was gone, Paul Bunyan picked Sourdough Sam up by the collar and marched him down the road to the widow-woman's house. After tapping politely with his little finger on the door, the giant lumberjack thrust Sam in

PAUL BUNYAN AND THE WITCH

front of the startled witch and made him apologize for his rude behavior toward her. Then the massive man crouched down and spoke at length with the witch, finally drawing her a map in the snow. When they finished their conversation, Paul Bunyan frog-marched Sourdough Sam back to camp and made him copy the words "I will not court witches ever again" a thousand times in the snow behind the bunkhouse.

After Sam finished his copying, he went cautiously over to the giant stove and lit it. The fire took hold instantly, and soon the stove was good and hot and flapjacks were sizzling on the griddle. Dinner was a merry meal, with hot pancakes and bacon and biscuits dripping with butter.

As he filled his plate, Johnny Inkslinger said to Paul Bunyan, "What did you say to that witch to get her to lift the curse on Sourdough Sam?"

Paul Bunyan chuckled. "I just told her about a man I met while I was out hunting for new timberland," he said. "His name is Herman the Hermit. He lives on the other side of Ironwood, and he is hankering for a wife. The witch-woman couldn't pack her bags fast enough!"

"Don't seem fair to poor Herman, sending him a witch woman who can't cook to be his wife," said Johnny.

"Not at all," said Paul Bunyan with a big grin. "Herman don't care who he marries as long as she can keep house. And he doesn't have any teeth, so the only thing he can eat is possum stew!"

The lumberjacks all laughed and then got down to some serious eating. As for Sourdough Sam, he vowed then and there to stick to cooking and leave the courting up to the younger men. And that's just what he did.

20

The Loup Garou

DETROIT

Listen close to my story, *ma petite*, for it is about an evil man and a pious woman and the power of good over evil. It is also the story of the statue of the wolf that stands in the garden of our church and how it came to be there.

Jacques Morand was a tall, handsome man with flashing black eyes and a flowing black mustache. He was a *coureur de bois* by trade. The *coureur de bois* were free-spirited woodsmen, the first to explore this great land. They lived among the native tribes of North America, trapping and trading their way into history with their feats of courage, survival, and adventure.

But Jacques Morand had evil in his heart, and he did not always live as he ought.

One day, when he was traveling through this part of the country, he chanced to spy the beautiful and pious Genevieve Parent. She was a holy woman, a novitiate who had dedicated her life to poverty and good work. She was preparing to take the final vows of chastity, poverty, and obedience that would make her a nun when she met Jacques Morand.

The *coureur de bois* was immediately infatuated with the beautiful young woman, and he tried to persuade her to give up the church and elope with him. Genevieve was adamant in her refusal. She had dedicated herself to the church and wanted nothing to do with this scoundrel. But Jacques Morand was not discouraged. He dearly loved a challenge, and he was determined to have Genevieve for his wife. He laid siege to the beautiful novitiate, showering her with gifts and flowers and serenading her at night when the good nuns were trying to sleep.

Monsieur le Curé—the priest of the parish—did everything he could to spare the poor Genevieve from the attention of her unwanted suitor. But the priest was a gentle man who had renounced violence when he took his vows, and his words had no effect on the evil Jacques Morand. One day, when the priest stood at the church door and denied the woodsman entrance to the room where Genevieve and the sisters were praying, the *coureur de bois* smashed the face of Monsieur le Curé with his fist, injuring him severely. The doctor was called to minister to the priest, and word was sent to the commander of the fort regarding the errant behavior of Jacques Morand. A troop of soldiers was dispatched to guard the good sisters and bar the *coureur de bois* from the church and convent.

Foiled in his attempt to seduce the pious Genevieve, Jacques decided to steal her away. He went deep into the woods to a place where witches dwell, and he implored them to come to his aid. At midnight, a dark crone with a humped back and a twisted face hobbled into the clearing where he waited beside a small fire. She listened impassively to his request for aid in abducting the pious maiden. Then she pointed her walking stick at the fire. At once, it blazed up higher and higher until the flames licked at the overhanging tree branches and scorched the skin of the *coureur de bois*.

"What will you give me in payment for rendering such aid?" the old crone shrieked as Jacques scrambled backward to avoid the searing heat and the flames.

"You may have my soul," the *coureur de bois* said bravely, throwing an arm in front of his face to shield him from the blazing light.

"Done!" said the witch. At once the fire went out. Jacques blinked several times in the sudden darkness and then gasped when he found himself gazing directly into the glowing red eyes of a giant wolf. There were still sparkles in his vision from the bright fire, and it took him a moment to realize that the creature held a small glass bottle in its teeth. It leaned toward him, offering him the bottle. Hesitantly, he took it.

Then the wolf spoke in the voice of the old crone. "Drink every drop of the potion in this bottle. It will allow you to turn at will into a wolf and back." To demonstrate, the wolf transformed itself into the crooked form of the old crone. For a moment, she leered at Jacques with her twisted face. Then she began to laugh, cackling louder and louder until the *coureur de bois* cowered, covering his ears and closing his eyes. And then there was silence, and Jacques found himself alone in the dark clearing with the glass bottle tucked into his pocket.

Jacques took the bottle into shaking hands, drew forth the cork, and drank its contents in one huge gulp. He felt it running through his body like fire, reaching every nerve and muscle within him. Gasping in pain, he curled up in a tight ball on the ground until the fire in his body flickered and went out. Cautiously, he straightened, wondering if he could really turn into a wolf. Even as he had the thought, his body convulsed once sharply in a moment of agony worse than that he had experienced when he drank the potion. And then he was viewing the world through the keen eyes of a gray wolf. He could see every detail of the clearing as if it were brightest day. When he moved, he felt the tug and flow of rippling muscles and the wind whistling gently through his fur. It was the most glorious moment of freedom he had ever experienced. Feeling nothing but elation, Jacques the *loup garou* loped through the night woods, his mind already miles ahead at the convent where Genevieve lay sleeping in her cell.

It was full daylight when the werewolf reached the church, so he hid himself in the underbrush and watched for an opportunity to seize the girl and drag her away. His moment came at dusk, when Genevieve walked alone in the convent garden behind the church. The soldier at the entrance to the walled garden nodded to her, allowing her inside since the last patrol had found the garden free of intruders. The *loup garou* waited in the shadows until the guards were at the other end of their patrol and then leapt easily over the large wall and landed softly on the grass within.

Silently, he stalked the beautiful novitiate as she walked reflectively through the garden, her attitude one of piety and prayer. Though he made no noise, some sixth sense alerted the girl to her danger. She looked up sharply, her eyes darting into every shadow. The *loup garou* froze behind the bushes, his body invisible to even the most experienced hunter. Genevieve shook her head slightly, as if she were mistaken, and resumed her walk. But her pace had quickened, and she moved with purpose.

The werewolf hurried after her, no longer troubling to keep to the shadows. He knew he must capture her quickly before she escaped through the garden door on the far side

THE LOUP GAROU

of the wall. But Genevieve has seen him stalking her and she started running, grasping her rosary tightly with one hand as she screamed for help. The *loup garou* bounded ahead of her and stopped between the novitiate and the iron gate leading out of the garden.

With a gasp of terror Genevieve halted and then ran into a little alcove in which stood a small fountain surrounded by a tiled patio. An ornate nook carved into the wall behind the fountain contained a beautiful statue of the Virgin Mary. Genevieve fell at the feet of the statue, begging the Virgin to come to her aid.

Behind her, the werewolf stalked into the alcove. It stared at her for a long moment and then transformed into the tall, handsome form of Jacques Morand. Passionately, the *coureur de bois* proclaimed his love for the girl, begging her to come to him of her own free will. Genevieve spurned him loudly, turning her face toward the statue of the Virgin and refusing to look at him.

In a fury, Jacques transformed back into a *loup garou* and sprang at the kneeling girl. Genevieve raised her arms to protect herself, her gaze locked with that of the beast. But in midair the werewolf turned to stone. Its frozen body clattered onto the tile patio, and its snarling head landed on the novitiate's legs.

At that moment, the gate to the garden burst open and several soldiers ran into the alcove. Summoned by Genevieve's screams, they had run silently along the outside of the wall while Jacques made his final pleas to the fair maiden. Now they stared in amazement at the statue of the springing wolf that lay on its side across the lower half of the frightened novitiate's body, searching in vain for a sign of the man they had heard accosting her moments before.

Two soldiers moved the heavy statue off the bruised girl, and another soldier helped Genevieve to her feet. She told the men what had happened and it was acknowledged by all to be a miracle, granted by the goodness of the Virgin Mary. The story soon spread throughout the community, and many people came to see the statue of the *loup garou*, which was set up in the Virgin's alcove as a reminder to all of the power of good over evil.

The pious Genevieve Parent went on to become a nun. In a few years, she was made abbess of the convent, where her good works and generous heart touched many lives up until the day she died.

21

The Wizard's Rope

PORT HURON

I'd left my old ship at Port Huron—creative disagreement with the captain—and spent a few weeks living off my earnings and taking in the sights. I'd grown up in this town and had become a sailor as soon as I found a captain who would sign me on as cabin boy. Solid ground makes me nervous. So when I'd finished blowing my money on the usual pursuits—wine, women, and gambling—I signed on with an old-world captain heading to Chicago.

Now old-world captains—top-ranking sailors that migrated to the States from seafaring countries around the globe—have a pretty stern reputation on the Great Lakes. They were real efficient and could pinch a dime until it cried for mercy. The ship owners loved them, but the crew didn't always agree. They were ambitious and worked so hard they often won jobs over the local boys, who consequently resented them. And you couldn't beat them when it came to making a fast run through the lakes from Oswego to Milwaukee. Folks claimed they were wizards who knew how to control the winds and the storms, but I figured that was a lot of hogwash. Sour grapes from some of the mates who thought they'd make captain first, and had been mistaken.

I loved my new ship—she was a brand-new 201-foot-long, three-masted schooner carrying a cargo of iron ore—and I quickly grew to admire her captain. There would be no creative differences here. I'd tow the line like every man jack aboard or get tossed into the frigid waters of the lake. The water was as flat as a pancake, and we made Chicago in record time.

I decided to stick with the ship awhile longer and was back onboard well before sailing time. We were halfway up Lake Michigan when the wind died away altogether, and the ship was becalmed in the middle of nowhere. I was ready with a whistle and a few silver coins in my pocket—a time-honored sailor's practice for calling a wind—but the first mate laid a hand on my arm and told me to wait. I found the mate's order strange until I looked around and saw everyone else waiting too, their eyes fixed on the captain's cabin.

All work had ceased, and tension mounted on the deck, releasing only when our stern captain strolled up on deck in his spankin' new uniform with a knotted rope in his hands and went to the bow of the ship. As we watched, the old man slowly unraveled one of the small knots at the top of the rope. Instantly a breeze sprang up, filling the sails and throwing the crew into a frenzy of work adjusting the ropes and canvas. I watched the captain surreptitiously as I worked and saw him release a few more knots while the wind built up slowly around us. Then we were sailing north and gaining speed with each moment that passed. The captain barked out a few commands and retired to his cabin with the rope.

THE WIZARD'S ROPE

I was a bit spooked by what I had seen. I thought all that talk about wizards was a lot of hokum, but I had no other explanation for what I had just seen. Our captain had just used an ordinary knotted rope to call the winds.

I asked the first mate about it, privately, when our watch was over. He treated the whole matter quite casually, as if it were quite normal to sail under a "Master of the Winds"—what we call a sailor-wizard.

"You should see the old man when there's a storm brewing," he said with a grin.

I smiled weakly in return, vowing that I would get off this ship as soon as I could. Who knows what a wizard would do to you if you ever crossed him? If the captain could control the winds and the storms, what other things . . . or creatures . . . could he summon out of the depths? I decided to ship off when we reached Port Huron.

We were nearing our destination when a mighty squall rose up out of nowhere. As soon as the mate saw the roiling black clouds on the horizon, he went running for the captain. The storm was coming on fast, and the swells were already rolling the ship from side to side when the captain went forward to the bow with his rope. He jerked two large knots apart fast and a huge wind slammed away from the ship, heading out toward the storm. I saw the wind smash directly into the clouds, driving them backward. For a moment, the storm wind and the captain's wind fought with one another, and the sea beneath them churned and whirled. A waterspout descended from the fighting clouds and I drew in my breath sharply, fearing for my life.

At the bow of the ship, the captain released a third large knot near the bottom of the rope, and a second wind raced away toward the storm. When this wind hit the storm clouds, they began to recede, heading toward Canada. Lake Huron was choppy and hard to manage for the next few hours, but the fierce squall had disappeared into the distance and the danger was gone. The first mate gave me a knowing grin as I passed, and I nodded to him. I no longer wondered why the men sailed with an Old World wizard. A man who could chase away a Great Lakes squall with a few twists of his fingers would earn any sailor's loyalty. Right then and there, I changed my mind about leaving.

The captain's wife joined the ship when we sailed out of Buffalo, and I'd never met a sterner, more forbidding woman in my life. Most men would have fled in terror before such a lady, but she seemed to suit the captain. I wondered if she knew that he was a wizard, but I never saw him bring out the rope after she came aboard, so I decided that she did not.

I thought things were strict under our captain, but I saw I was wrong. No one dared step one inch out of line when the wife was onboard. The men doffed their caps when she went by and said "please" and "thank you" in the mess, even when she wasn't present. They even stopped swearing.

I cussed just once after she came aboard, and the lecture I got in manners from that formidable lady rang in my ears for hours. The crew gave me sympathetic smiles all that day. I realized that this sort of thing had happened before to the new man onboard; a kind of sailor's initiation rite.

"You should'a warned me," I complained to the mate, but he just gave me his cheeky grin.

"Best to learn these things for yourself," he said.

"Ha!" I said to his retreating back, but he just hummed merrily under his breath and went to check the rigging.

The captain's wife was appallingly clean. I thought the ship was in good shape when we arrived in Buffalo, but the lady was not pleased. I spent most of my waking hours scrubbing the decks; yet somehow she always found a spot I'd missed.

We sailed across Lake Erie, threaded our way through Lake St. Clare and the St. Clare River, and then were out on Lake Huron and pulling into my home port. By then, I was sorely tempted to abandon ship, since I wasn't sure how much more I could take of the captain's wife. Still, I would probably never find a safer ship in all my born days, and the mate assured me that she took only one trip onboard the ship each year. So I stayed aboard, and a few days later we left Port Huron and set sail up the lake, heading for Chicago.

We were only a few hours out of port when the captain's wife approached his quarters with a broom and a mop. Up until that period, the captain had managed to keep his wife from doing more than a cursory clean-up in his quarters and had forbade her to enter the private alcove where he kept all the ship's records (and, I suspected, his wizardly tools). But the look she gave her husband would have cowed a stronger man than our captain. He retreated with as much dignity as possible and went to inspect the below-decks.

With the captain and his lady both occupied, things were quite peaceful up on deck. Until the first of the winds arrived, whooshing out of the captain's door and wrapping around us before taking off up into the sky. The ship lurched as the rising winds competed with those currently filling our sails. But there was more to come.

Fierce storm winds shuddered forth from the cabin; whirlwinds and roaring nor'easters. Around me, men were shouting and grabbing onto anything they could hold. Two blokes were swept off their feet and right over the side of the ship as I staggered forward against the hurricane-force wind that was spinning the ship around and around in circles. I managed to catch hold of the door to the captain's quarters. Inside, I saw that woman undoing the last of the knots in the rope, the big one on the bottom.

"No!" I shouted, but it was too late. The knot came undone, and the winds from a thousand gales that had been tied into that knot were released all at one go. The ship exploded under the fierce onslaught, and I felt myself tossed high into the air, both hands still gripping the captain's door. Then something struck me in the head and everything went black.

I came to my senses many hours later, surprised to be alive, and found that I was floating half on and half off the captain's door, held there by the buttons of my jacket, which had become jammed into the hinge. Thank God for those buttons, I thought fervently, knowing that I would have sunk to the bottom of the lake and drowned without them.

There was no sign of my ship, and what debris surrounded me was very small indeed. The waves I was coasting upon were still rough in the aftermath of the windy onslaught, but the sky was crystal clear above me. I dragged myself on top of the door and rode the waves to the shores of Michigan, arriving on a sandy spit much more quickly than I would have expected.

I lay on the beach next to the captain's door until some of my strength returned. Then I hotfooted it for Port Huron, only a few miles south of my landing place. I made my way to the home of my cousin, who took me in and tidied me up. He was pleased to learn the cause of the mysterious windstorm that had swept the coast a few hours before, and he agreed that I was lucky to be alive. We decided it would be best if I didn't tell the whole truth about the shipwreck. Folks might get nervous if they found out that there really were "Masters of the Wind" out there.

It took me a month to recover my nerve, but after that I signed on with another ship and was back out on the lakes. You can be sure my captain had been born in America. I wasn't taking any chances with old-world captains ever again.

22

Doppelganger

LANSING

"It's been years since I thought of Granny," old Jack Bennett said to his great-grandson with a cheerful grin. "What a gal! What a gal!"

"Hang on, Grandpa. I want to record this," Jack Bennett the fourth said, turning on the tiny machine he held in his hand.

Old Jack peered at it through his oversized glasses. "Is that another one of your crazy devices?" he asked suspiciously.

"It's a digital recorder. After I tape your story, I can plug the recorder right into the computer, download the audio file, and burn it to disk. You can listen to it yourself on a CD!" Jack the fourth said.

"I don't want to listen to myself on a CD," old Jack said testily. "Do you or do you not want to hear this story?"

Jack the fourth laughed and settled back into the chair. "As I recall, Grandpa, you were the one who called and asked me to come over today with a recorder. You claimed it was urgent."

"Well, it is urgent," said old Jack. "I've got one more story for your collection, and if you don't take it down today, you won't get another chance."

"Nonsense, Grandpa," Jack the fourth said. "The doctor says you're fit as a fiddle and will be with us until you're one hundred."

Old Jack shook his head, but he didn't argue with his great-grandson. Instead, he told the following story.

The week before I turned eight, Granny came to live with us. She was the oldest person I'd ever seen. She had white hair that was curled in ringlets all over her head. Her blue eyes were sunken in and hard to see around the wrinkles in her face. Her hands were crippled with arthritis, and the blue veins popped out of them whenever she gripped her cane. She walked with a stoop, and when she laughed, she cackled like a witch.

"Come give your old Granny a hug, Jacky," she said when she saw me watching her from the porch. I didn't like being called Jacky. I was a tough little kid who played baseball with the other boys and raced around all day gathering toads and snakes and other useful items for scaring the girls. But I went over and hugged her anyway, then told her I preferred to be called Jack. She laughed her witch's cackle and gave me a lemon drop.

At the time, I figured she was at least two hundred years old, but my parents told me later that she was eighty-nine, which was quite an advanced age for that time. In spite of her ancient appearance, Granny had the spirit of a young girl. She'd waltz across the kitchen with her cane, and she'd make me play baseball with her. She got quite good at batting, but I'd have to run the bases for her.

Sometimes at night, she'd stand before the ornate, full-length mirror in her room and shout "Doppelganger!" and then start cackling her witch's laugh. I jumped the first time I heard her shout, and hurried into the bedroom, sure something was wrong.

"See my doppelganger, Jacky," she said, pointing at her reflection in the mirror.

"What's a 'doppelganger'?" I asked, staring at her suspiciously.

"It's a German word," Granny said. "It means 'double walker.' It's your phantom self, your shadow that follows you everywhere. If you ever see your doppelganger outside of a reflection, it means that death is nearby!"

She said this quite cheerfully. Granny was never afraid of death. She looked on it as the next step in her growth as a human being. "I'm gonna have me a new body, Jacky," she'd say. "One where my back doesn't ache and my hands aren't so ugly and twisted. I'll be able to knock a baseball right over the garden fence once I've passed on!"

Mama didn't like it when Granny talked about death, but I didn't mind at all. The way Granny described it, death and its aftermath sounded like a wonderful adventure.

About six months after Granny moved into our house, I was standing in the doorway to the porch, watching the fireflies as dusk settled over the trees and bushes in our yard. I was eating an ice cream cone and listening to Granny humming to herself as she rocked back and forth in her rocker by the fireplace.

All at once, Granny appeared right before me, walking briskly along the porch toward the front steps. I could see her, clear as day as she hobbled down the stairs, cane in hand. But from the corner of my eye, I could also see her rocking in her chair. I gasped aloud. "Doppelganger," I shouted without stopping to think.

Granny's doppelganger hurried along the walkway and through the front gate. I ran after her, ice cream dripping everywhere. By the time I reached the fence, the doppelganger was gone. I stared around in the growing darkness for a moment, until I realized my hand was cold and sticky with melting ice cream. Recalled to myself, I licked at the rapidly disappearing treat and walked back inside the house.

Granny looked up from her chair when I entered. "You're a mess, Jacky," she said. "You've got ice cream all over you!"

"Granny, I just saw your doppelganger," I said, wiping ineffectively at the ice cream on my shirt.

"I'm not surprised," Granny said. "I've been seeing her all day."

"Isn't it bad luck to see someone's doppelganger?" I asked, stuffing the last bit of ice cream cone in my mouth and wiping my hands on my already-dirty shirt.

"It usually means that person is going to die," Granny said matter-of-factly. "And about time too," she added briskly. "I'm sick of this tired old body. Can't wait to get the new one. I'll be hitting the baseball right over the fence in no time, Jacky."

Her words gave me an odd feeling in my chest. I'd grown to love this wrinkled old lady, and I didn't like the thought of her going away. Granny read my face like a book. "Now don't you get all sad on me, Jacky. I'm happy to be joining your Granddaddy in heaven. But I won't be too far from you. Not ever. You'll see."

Granny died in her sleep that night, with a great big smile on her face. I was a tough little boy, but I cried like a baby at her

DOPPELGANGER

funeral. I missed her something terrible, and took no comfort in her last words to me. She seemed very far away indeed, and I wished she'd stayed in her old wrinkled body instead of putting on a new one.

I was outside staring listlessly at my bat and ball while the grown-ups wept and ate at the reception my parents held at our house after the funeral. Suddenly, the bat and ball rose up in the air all by themselves. The ball was tossed up, the bat swung, and CRACK! The ball flew up and away over the fence.

I stared in amazement as the bat fell to the ground. There came the sound of running footsteps, and suddenly I saw a semi-transparent young girl who looked like a younger version of Granny running around the makeshift bases in the backyard. When she reached home plate, she threw up her arms triumphantly, did a little victory dance, gave me a huge grin, and disappeared.

That was the very last time I ever saw Granny. But from that moment on, I knew in my heart as well as my head that she would never be far away from me. And she never was.

Old Jack leaned back in his chair, exhausted by the telling of his story. Jack the fourth snapped off the digital recorder, his eyes shining brightly.

"Wow, Grandpa," he exclaimed. "What a great story."

"Yes," old Jack agreed with a smile. "And there is a sequel."

Jack the fourth blinked. "You saw her again?" he asked.

"No. I didn't see Granny again," said old Jack. "But I did see another doppelganger."

"A doppelganger?" Jack the fourth asked. "Whose? When? Where?"

"This morning," old Jack said, "when I came back to my room after breakfast. I looked out the bedroom window and I saw my doppelganger walk through the front door of the nursing home and out along the street."

Jack the fourth gasped. "No, Grandpa. You must be mistaken!"

"No mistake," said old Jack. "That's why I called you." He took a deep breath and smiled at his beloved great-grandson. "I wanted you to hear one last story from your Grandpa, so you wouldn't be sad when I pass on. Just like my Granny told me, I'm telling you: I won't be too far from you. Not ever."

Old Jack reached out and patted his great-grandson's hand. "You'll see."

23

The Nain Rouge

DETROIT

Pierre sat beside the rain-streaked window, staring out into the darkness. It was a dark and stormy night; a night suited perfectly for this deathwatch, he thought gloomily. Naturally. His sister Josette had a knack for arranging everything in the most suitable manner, from what she wore to the appropriate weather. It was a trait that drove him crazy—especially when what she tried to arrange was his life.

Pierre had long ago come to grips with the fact that he was a harum-scarum kind of person—the sort who changed his mind on the slightest whim. His flightiness hadn't helped him hold a job, but it had given him an exciting life.

Now Josette lay dying in her bed, dressed in a perfectly pressed nightgown adorned with lace and ruffles. A blue nightcap framed her tightly curled white hair, and she held a Bible in her hand. Outside, thunder rumbled, lightning flashed, and rain pounded in a suitably grim and foreboding manner.

Pierre sighed a little, and Josette called to him from the bed. "Stop sighing like a ninny," she said. "Straighten up and act sensibly for once in your life, Pierre. And come over here where

149

I can see you. You are the only relation I have left in this world, and you should be at my side when my time comes."

Pierre bit back a sharp retort, something he would not have done if Josette hadn't been on her deathbed, and went to his sister's side. He hated it when she ordered him around. From the day he was born, Josette had been trying to make him as perfect as she was, and she still had not succeeded. This annoyed her greatly, and was probably the reason she was being so stubborn about the mill.

As he took her thin, cold hand in his, Pierre almost forgave her for the long debates they'd had lately over the running of the mill. Almost a year ago he had come home penniless from the West, having sunk everything he owned into a gold mine that went bust. At that time, he had told his sister that he was tired of adventuring and was going to settle down and work in the family mill. His sister was not happy with the arrangement, but she could say little about it since their parents had left them equal shares in the business. Pierre had worked hard during the next few months, learning the business from top to bottom, and he had earned the respect of Henry Smith, the supervisor his sister had hired to run the mill after her husband's death.

When the doctor told his sister that she had only a few months left to live, Pierre had asked her if she would leave her half of the mill to him. Josette had promptly told him no. Her half of the mill was going to Henry Smith, the current supervisor, whom she had hand-picked for the job and who was twice the man that her brother ever could be. And from that position she would not budge, no matter how they argued.

"Pierre, you are woolgathering," Josette snapped weakly, frowning at him from her pillow. "Honestly, can't you behave in a respectable manner just this once? You should be comforting me in my final hours. It's a good thing I didn't leave you my half of the mill. You'd bankrupt the whole operation in under a year!"

Pierre was indignant. Henry Smith had commended his work to Josette time and again, but she never believed the supervisor's reports. "That's not fair, Josette," he said as calmly as he could. "I have worked hard to learn the business ever since I got home, and I am quite competent. I would keep the mill profitable and I would keep Henry Smith as supervisor, just the way you want it. Mother and Father wanted the mill to remain in the family."

"Mother and Father would have been terribly disappointed in you if they'd lived," Josette snapped, "just as I have been. I'd rather leave the mill to the devil than to you!"

As the words left her mouth, a bolt of lightning flashed down from the clouds and crashed into a tree near the house with a loud boom and a burst of electricity that made Pierre's hair stand on end. He leapt to his feet and ran to the window, his eyes still tingling from the bright glare. As he reached the window, he heard a rat-a-tat-tat sound, and suddenly a grotesque face appeared on the other side of the glass. A shambling, red-skinned creature leered at him. It had horribly decaying teeth, a twisted nose, and cold, glittering eyes. Behind its head, Pierre could see the old oak tree smoldering in the lashing rain, part of its trunk sheared clean off by the lightning bolt.

The strange red gremlin made a rude gesture with its hand and dropped away from the window. In the next flash of lightning, Pierre saw the red dwarf turning cartwheels along the walkway. For a moment, he lost sight of it in the darkness

THE NAIN ROUGE

between the lightning flashes; then he spotted the creature one more time standing by the fence. It hopped up and down delightedly, gesturing first toward Pierre, then toward the south. It laughed at him and rubbed its hands with glee. Finally, it made another foul gesture and then disappeared into the rain-lashed lane, heading south.

Pierre stared into the darkness in shock, realizing that he had just seen the infamous Nain Rouge of Detroit. The red dwarf was called "The Demon of the Strait," and its appearance was said to herald disaster.

Cadillac, founder of Detroit, had been the first to encounter the Nain Rouge. While Cadillac was sitting on the bank of the Detroit River, the red dwarf had jumped out of a tree, landing right in front of the French Colonial governor, startling him nearly out of his wits. The twisted creature had brandished a long stick as if it were a sword. It gave the governor several painful whacks before the startled man recovered enough to draw his own sword and parry the attack. He managed to beat the creature back with the flat of his blade. Finally, the red dwarf broke off its mock attack and ran away, cackling madly to itself all the while.

Cadillac thought no more of the strange encounter until other things started to go wrong. Bad luck plagued him at every turn, and all of his schemes seemed to go awry. He managed to upset the Montreal traders, turn the Jesuits against him, and anger the governor of New France. Eventually he was recalled to France, losing his trade monopoly and all of his privileges. Ever afterward, he blamed his failure in the New World on the Nain Rouge.

But this was just the first of many disasters attributed to the satanic imp. Pierre recalled the story of Blood Run, a battle between the British soldiers holding Fort Detroit and Pontiac's group of rebel Native American tribes. After the united tribes had attacked a number of settlements and laid siege to Fort Detroit, the British attempted to end the siege with a sneak attack on Pontiac's encampment. But their plan was revealed to the rebel leader, and Pontiac defeated the British in the Battle of Blood Run, which took place at a creek 2 miles north of the fort. Several survivors of the battle claimed to have seen the red dwarf running along the shores of the lake shortly before the battle began.

The imp was spotted once again in 1805, racing through the streets of Detroit just before the city burned to the ground. And during the War of 1812, when the forces of British General Brock began bombarding the American forces within Fort Detroit, the American general acceded to a demand for unconditional surrender after he saw the Nain Rouge leering at him through the fog.

And now Pierre himself had seen the creature, just after Josette had made her pronouncement about leaving the mill to the devil! Pierre's heart almost stopped when he realized that the Nain Rouge had headed south when he left their house—straight toward the family mill.

From the bed, Josette was loudly demanding to know why Pierre had left her side. She gasped and clutched her heart dramatically. Pierre strained his eyes southward, trying to see where the imp had gone, but he could make out nothing except the whipping wind, the pouring rain, and the occasional flash of lightning.

Josette called to him again, and Pierre pushed aside his fears and hurried over to the bed. He took Josette's hand, determined not to burden his sister with his worries in her last hours. He had always been a good brother to Josette, ignoring her disapproving attitude as best he could, and so he said nothing further about the mill. Instead, he talked about the happy childhood memories they shared, about what a good wife Josette had been, and other cheerful topics. Josette's final hours were spent in peace, with accord between the two siblings. Pierre even wept a little when she passed, although he knew she was ready to join her husband in the hereafter.

After leaving his sister's body to the care of the undertaker, Pierre hurried back to his house in the early-morning drizzle, worrying about the strange appearance of the Nain Rouge. It obviously had not come to claim Josette herself, for a more pious woman had never lived. No. Its appearance must have something to do with the mill.

Suddenly, Pierre realized that he could smell smoke in the air. Something big was burning and had been for quite a while. He raced to his small stable, saddled his horse, and rode as fast as he could toward the mill.

He slowed his horse when he reached the top of the hill and looked down upon the blackened ruins that had once been the family mill. It was obviously far too late to do anything about the fire. The flames were out, though some parts of the building were still smoking and the firefighters were watching the hot spots. Henry Smith, who lived next door to the mill, had managed to save only a few pieces of equipment before the fire consumed the building.

When Henry saw Pierre ride into the mill yard, he came to speak to him. "It was the strangest thing you ever saw," the supervisor said, mopping his face with a blackened handkerchief.

"The storm had already passed through this area when a bolt of lightning came out of nowhere and struck the mill early this morning. I was walking out to my barn to milk our cow and saw the whole thing." By the time he had given the alarm and run to the mill, Henry said, the fire was already out of control.

The supervisor gazed at the scene of destruction sadly, and then inquired after Josette. Pierre told him that his sister had died in the night, and the supervisor nodded sadly. "I'm glad she passed before this happened," he said. "It would have broken her heart to know that all her hard work had gone up in flames."

The supervisor excused himself and walked over to a knot of men who were checking to make sure the fire was completely out. He began giving instructions for clearing away the debris and moving the saved items into his barn until they could decide what to do with them.

Pierre turned his horse around and started back toward home. As his horse stepped onto the bridge spanning the mill stream, his eye was caught by movement near the water. To his dismay, he saw the Red Dwarf tugging on the fire-blackened mill wheel as if he were trying to get it started. The creature looked over toward Pierre and gave him a foul, drooling grin and a cocky wave. Then it danced away down the bank of the stream, turning cartwheels and cackling to itself.

After the destruction of the mill and two sightings of the ill-omened Nain Rouge, Pierre figured he didn't stand a chance of making a living in Detroit. Right after his sister's funeral, he sold his house, took the money he'd earned working in the mill, and headed back out west.

24

The Seagull

The men in our family have been Great Lakes sailors for generations. Members of our family like to say that we have lake water running in our veins instead of blood. My great-great-granddaddy started out as a commercial fisherman, and each generation followed in his footsteps until my father broke with tradition and became a "salty"; traveling across the Great Lakes, through the Saint Lawrence River, and out to sea. I took a job on one of the "lakers"—a Lakes bulk freighter—as soon as I got enough schooling, and worked my way up to captain as fast as I could.

My home port was Detroit in those days, though I did not see my home or my wife nearly as much as I would have liked. But she never complained—she was a true captain's wife. We had one child, a boy, who inherited the family love of the water. He was a better sailor than I by the time he was ten, and my wife and I were very proud when he joined the Coast Guard.

I had married late and was getting on in years by the time our boy was grown. I'd squirreled away enough money to retire early. It was not long after Charlie started his career on the Lakes that I ended mine, much to the quiet relief of my wife.

I'd survived one too many lake hurricanes, and we both knew I was lucky to have lived to old age.

During the early spring, the wife and I packed up our things and moved north to Traverse City. We still had access to a commercial deep water port, and I ran a commercial fishing boat out onto Lake Michigan a few times a week when the mood struck me. But mostly we relaxed, getting to know our new community, enjoying our retirement, and watching Charlie's career with pride.

Then one summer evening, I came home from a good day's fishing to find my wife waiting for me on the dock. Her body was tense with emotion and her eyes far away. Something in her attitude triggered a long-buried memory. Before my mind's eye flashed a vision: little tow-headed Charlie, age three, slipping on the deck of our sailboat and plunging over the side. I heard again his terrified cries as he flailed in the deep water and felt the chill of the cold water as I dove in beside him and pulled him to safety. The look on my wife's face that day, when she saw little Charlie plunge over the side of our boat, was the same look she had on her face now, and I knew before I reached her that Charlie was dead. He'd been swept overboard in a storm and drowned.

I'm not too sure how we got by in the days that followed. Charlie was our only child, and my wife and I were devastated by his loss. About two weeks after the funeral, I came home from fishing to find my wife standing out on the back deck, her eyes fixed on something in the backyard. She didn't even glance at me as I joined her at the rail; she just pointed toward the water. I followed her gesture and saw a ring-billed seagull standing on the huge, rusted ship's anchor that stood beside the

THE SEAGULL

little dock where we kept my wife's sailboat. It had been a gift to us from Charlie, who'd retrieved it from a shipwreck during one of his diving vacations.

There was nothing remarkable about the bird, save for a funny dark-gray patch on one of its light-gray wings. But it stood unnaturally still, and its bright eyes were fixed on us as if it wanted to speak. Like all sailors, I was fond of seagulls. Their bodies are said to contain the souls of drowned sailors who come back to help the living. Whenever a seagull landed on my fishing boat, I took it as a good omen. I'd brought home many a fine catch and sailed safely through many a rough sea accompanied by a seagull companion.

This bird seemed different from the other gulls I'd seen all my life; more intense somehow, as if it truly contained a living soul. After considering me for a moment, the seagull opened its beak and cried out plaintively. My heart began beating faster. The seagull's voice sounded just like the voice of my son Charlie.

"It flew right into the house through the front window," my wife said, her voice breaking. "It perched on the back of Charlie's favorite chair and called out to me in Charlie's voice. Then it sailed out the back door and it's been sitting on Charlie's anchor ever since. I think it's been waiting for you to come home."

Hearing her voice, the seagull called again and then flew toward us, settling on the railing. My wife began to tremble. "Charlie?" she whispered. The seagull blinked its eyes at her, bobbed its head once, and then flew in a circle around us before heading out over the lake. It disappeared into the sunset, and my wife sighed softly, as if a weight had lifted from her shoulders.

From that moment, my wife's spirits began to pick up, and a little of the shadow passed from her face.

The seagull with the funny gray patch took up residence on our anchor after that, and my wife took comfort in its presence, often bringing out slices of her homemade bread to feed it after our evening meal. The seagull would accompany her out on the sailboat, and she spoke to it as if it were the spirit of our son Charlie returned to comfort her.

About two months after Charlie's death, I was out fishing by myself a couple of miles offshore when I heard a familiar cry. Looking up, I saw my wife's seagull flying quickly toward me over the choppy waves. It perched on the bow and called out "Ma, Ma," in Charlie's voice. I was alarmed and turned the boat at once, sure that something had happened to my wife. "I'm coming, Charlie," I said to the bird. The seagull bobbed its head and flew back toward shore. I gunned the motor and followed it.

I made it back to the harbor in record time and broke all the speeding laws driving back to the house. I shouted for my wife as I crashed through the front door, but there was no answer. I searched the downstairs for her and then heard the seagull's voice from the backyard: "Ma, Ma!"

I ran out the back door and found my wife unconscious on the ground beneath our deck with the seagull huddled next to her broken right arm. A shattered flowerpot beside her and the broken deck railing above revealed what had happened. I was afraid to move her, so I commanded the seagull to stay with her and ran to telephone for an ambulance. Then the bird and I crouched beside my wife, one on either side of her, until the wail of a siren indicated that help had arrived.

At the hospital, it was found that my wife had sustained severe internal damage from the fall, and she was rushed into surgery. It was a close thing. The doctor told me in the recovery ward that I'd arrived just in time. In another half hour, she would have been too far gone for him to save her.

I didn't get home to my empty house until midnight. Before going to bed, I hurried to Charlie's anchor out back. The seagull was perched there with its head under its wing. It looked up as I approached and called out: "Ma, Ma?"

"Ma's going to be alright," I told it. "Thank you, Charlie."

The bird fluffed its feathers in delight and blinked its eyes several times.

Then it opened its beak and called again. I know it sounds crazy, but I swear there were words in its cry. It sounded like the bird said "Love you. Love you."

Tears sprang to my eyes. "We love you too," I said as the seagull sprang from its perch on the anchor and flew out over the darkened waters of Lake Michigan.

We never saw the seagull again.

My wife recovered fully and came home a month later. To this day, we both believe that Charlie's spirit came back to us for a few weeks to comfort and protect his mother, and went away again after he knew she was safe.

25

Nishishin Raises the Dead

MACKINAC ISLAND

There once was a cantankerous old man who had a fair daughter named Shaningo, which means "beautiful one." Every warrior for miles around dreamed of winning the hand of the maiden, but few dared approach her because of the fearsome reputation of her father.

Now Shaningo was enamored with a handsome young warrior named Nishishin. They had been friends since childhood, and one beautiful summer their friendship was transformed by the glorious fires of love. They wooed in secret, knowing that Shaningo's father would drive Nishishin away just as he had done every other suitor who had approached him. But they were reluctant to run away to be married, for they loved their island home and their people and wished to remain among them.

Now Nishishin was as wise and clever as he was handsome. It was his dream to become a great medicine man as well as a kind and generous husband. After much thought, he came up with a scheme that he knew would accomplish both his goals: to convince Shaningo's father of his worthiness and to persuade the medicine man that he should become his apprentice.

When Shaningo first heard his plan, she was skeptical. It was a good idea, she acknowledged, but would it be enough to bend the will of her fierce father? Still, the only other option was to leave her home and her family, so she agreed to help her beloved carry out his scheme.

The next evening, Nishishin appeared at her home and asked Shaningo's father if he might escort her to the tribal dance scheduled for that night. As predicted, the father was furious that anyone dared to approach his beautiful daughter. He drove Nishishin away with such harsh language and such loud cries that everyone in the village came to see what was wrong.

There were many indignant faces among the villagers when they saw how terribly Shaningo's father behaved toward the young man. But Nishishin faced him with a courage that did not waiver or turn to anger in the face of the abuse. His steadiness won him much favor in the village-fathers' eyes. The young man withdrew with dignity, exchanging a prolonged look with Shaningo as he left. This infuriated her father still further, but it endeared him to all those with romantic hearts in the village.

A dispirited Shaningo attended the dance in the company of her father that night. Over the next few days, she grew pale and wan and spent more and more of her time walking along the shores of the lake. Then one night, she did not return to her home. Her father was enraged, sure that the maiden had run away with Nishishin. He woke the whole village with his cries of rage as he ran to the lodge where Nishishin lived with his parents. But to his astonishment, Nishishin emerged from the dwelling by himself. Blinking sleepily, the young man denied any knowledge of Shaningo's disappearance. While her father searched the lodge in vain, the young warrior began pacing worriedly, obviously concerned about the safety of his beloved Shaningo.

The hearts of many were moved by his distress. Shaningo's father was scolded for his behavior and a search party was sent to seek out the maiden. At dawn, her blanket was discovered on the shores of the lake, and a beaded ornament she sometimes wore in her hair was found floating nearby. Nishishin gasped in dismay and wept aloud, sure that his darling had drowned in the lake.

Shaningo's father stood for a very long time holding the blanket in his hands, unable to speak. Then he turned abruptly on the tribe's medicine man and began berating him soundly. The medicine man should have foreseen this! He should have warned the family! Several warriors had to forcibly restrain him and sternly march him back to his wigwam.

Shaningo's father raged for days about her drowning, abusing the elders of his village so fiercely that the chief of the village was finally forced to threatened him with exile or execution if he did not control himself. Meanwhile, Nishishin became almost as pale and wan as his beloved Shaningo had been during the days that her father kept them apart. He spent much of his time by the shore, lighting small fires and praying to the spirits.

One day, two weeks after Shaningo's death, Nishishin appeared before the chief and elders of his tribe. He had been given a message from the spirit world. If he would brave the waters of the lake, swim down to the gods of the netherworld, and plead with them to return the beautiful and virtuous Shaningo, the maiden would be given into his keeping and restored to life as his wife. This he had vowed to do. It was a dangerous undertaking, but Nishishin felt that life was not worth living without Shaningo beside him, and he was determined to try.

The elders of his village reluctantly gave him permission to go. The whole village—even Shaningo's father—accompanied the young man to the water's edge. After bidding farewell to his weeping mother and grave-faced father, Nishishin leapt into the water and quickly disappeared beneath the surface. He was a strong swimmer, everyone knew, but surely even he could not survive for long deep beneath the waters of the lake.

One minute passed, then two. A few people who had been holding their breath since Nishishin plunged into the cold depths finally gasped, their faces red with strain. Three minutes passed. Then four, and five. Nishishin's mother began to wail softly, sure that her son had drowned. Another five minutes passed. Then ten. Those with a pessimistic nature turned away, shaking their heads at the foolishness of the young warrior who thought he could raise the dead.

Suddenly, Nishishin's mother cried out and pointed toward the water. Someone was swimming up to the surface—no, two people were. A moment later, Nishishin burst through the surface of the water, his arm around the waist of the beautiful maiden Shaningo. The girl was pale and thin, and her eyes had lost some of their sparkle. But she was alive and breathing and clinging to Nishishin as if he were her savior—which perhaps he was.

Shaningo's father gave a loud cry and dropped to his knees. To the surprise of all, tears were streaming down the face of the cantankerous old man. He ran into the water and caught Nishishin and Shaningo in an embrace, squeezing them both until they could barely breathe. Shaningo finally had to scold

NISHISHIN RAISES THE DEAD

him, warning him that he was about to send her back to the netherworld from which she had just emerged.

The father pulled the two young people from the water and had them married right there and then on the shore. He could not stop weeping, and he could not say enough good things about Nishishin, his beloved son-in-law who had returned life to his daughter.

From that moment on, whatever Nishishin said was law to Shaningo's father. He built the couple an enormous wigwam right next to his own, furnishing it with the very best of his property, all the while thanking his son-in-law for raising his daughter from the dead with every breath he took.

Nishishin was revered by his people as a holy man, and the tribal medicine man took the young man as his apprentice. Nishishin, happy with his lovely wife, a growing family, and a new profession, never told anyone his secret. But once each year, on the anniversary of her "resurrection," Nishishin and Shaningo would slip out of their wigwam and swim underneath the lake, through a short underwater tunnel and into the large cave that had once sheltered the maiden for two weeks. There they spent a romantic night together, cuddled up around a small fire, eating a special meal that Shaningo had prepared for them and rejoicing in the successful outcome of their plan.

26

The Dream

DEER PARK

The dream, when it came, was so vivid that at first Benjamin did not know that he dreamed. He was making his typical midnight patrol along the stretch of beach known as "shipwreck coast," something he did every night as he executed his duties as a surfman. Ben was one of several men who patrolled the beach each day, trying to prevent shipwrecks and save the lives of crewmen when a wreck did occur.

In his dream, Ben made his way through a screaming northern gale that drenched his skin, tore at his oilskins with whipping fingers of wind, and howled in his ears until it was hard to see or hear anything in the fearsome night. He had not traveled far from the station when he sensed, rather than saw, that he was not alone. Shaking the rain out of his eyes, Ben peered through the roaring darkness and saw a well-dressed man coming toward him out of the furious night. The stranger stopped in front of the surfman and began speaking. Strain his ears though he might, Ben could not hear the man over the massive bellow of the breakers pounding the shore.

Once, twice, three times the man gestured frantically toward the raging lake. He drew close to Ben in a final attempt to communicate, until his face was nearly pressed against that of the lone surfman. Then he vanished without a trace. Ben gasped in disbelief, his pulse pounding harder than the thundering of the waves. Then abruptly, he awoke.

For a long moment Ben lay sweating in terror on the bed and listening to the storm raging outside, convinced that the dream was an omen. Somewhere in the gale there was a ship that was about to sink to the bottom of the lake. But where was it? And when was it going to fail?

Frustrated, Ben pondered what to do. Old-timers claimed there was one shipwreck for every mile along the 40-mile stretch of Lake Superior's "shipwreck coast," and Ben knew that the bones of many a drowned sailor were buried deep beneath the long beach. Slowly, he dressed himself for duty as the surfmen currently on patrol returned to the station, sopping wet but cheerful to report a night free of wrecks.

Soberly, Ben repeated his dream to the crew. They laughed and told him to ignore it. Such dreams were part and parcel of the job, they said. Ben shook his head, but their words helped alleviate the burden he felt. Perhaps they were right. Rigged up, he shoved hard against the windswept door and staggered out into the storm.

Shoulders set against the howling wind and rain, Ben trudged along the 4-mile stretch of beach that was his patrol, stopping at the end to punch the time clock in the key post before turning and walking back again. He strained his eyes over the roaring breakers, searching for any sign of a ship in trouble, but he saw nothing out of the ordinary. Relieved, Ben reported a clear stretch of coast when he returned to the warmth and safety of the service station.

Ben and his fellow surfmen were gathered in the mess for the noon meal the next day when a battered, surf-beaten sailor staggered into the station. The men rushed to his aid, wrapping him in blankets and filling him with hot coffee. When the sailor had recovered a bit, he told his story.

The sailor's name was Harry Steward, and he was the wheelman of the steamer *Western Reserve*. The ship had been cruising for Duluth, Minnesota, the previous day when it rounded Whitefish Point and smacked headlong into the wind. The crew, longtime veterans of the Great Lakes, had kept the ship on course, not an easy task in the growing storm. The ship's owner, Captain Peter Minch, was aboard the *Western Reserve*, taking a trip with his wife and children. Although worried by the storm, Minch had every faith in the men he had chosen to sail his ship, and he managed to keep his young family calm.

Around 9:00 p.m., just 35 miles northeast of Deer Point, the steamer gave a strange heave and shuddered from stem to stern. Then, with a terrible jolt, the ship cracked open across her spar deck just in front of the boiler room. Knowing the *Western Reserve* was going down, the order was given to abandon ship. Twenty-one crewmen and six passengers, including the owner and his family, piled into two yawls and were launched into the raging seas.

The first yawl capsized almost immediately, throwing her passengers into the chilly water. Harry Steward was the sole survivor from the first yawl. He managed to swim to the other boat, which held the *Western Reserve*'s owner Peter Minch and his family, and he was pulled to safety by the remaining crew. They rowed away from the sinking ship as quickly as they could to avoid being pulled down in her wake. A few moments later, the *Western Reserve* sank without a trace beneath the waves, a mere ten minutes after she had cracked from the pressure of the storm.

For the next ten hours, the surviving crew members kept the bow of the yawl headed into the mountainous, boiling seas and bailed for dear life. Then, a mere mile off the beach, a massive series of breakers capsized the yawl. Once again, Steward found himself thrown into the roaring surf, fighting desperately to stay alive and afloat.

Through the howling storm, Steward could hear the wails of the children, the screams of the women, and the horrible moaning of the other crewmen. But the waves swept him relentlessly forward, and he had no way to reach any of the survivors. Slowly, the voices died away.

Steward, resigned to his own death, nonetheless continued to battle his way shoreward for the next two hours, finally tearing himself from the raging breakers of Lake Superior to collapse on the beach. Sooner than he wished, he pushed himself upright; calling upon previously unknown sources of strength to complete his journey to the life station to summon help, hoping against hope that others, like himself, had survived the wreck.

Upon hearing of the wreck, the keeper had immediately alerted the other life stations, and soon surfmen were swarming the beaches, searching for survivors. Ben was at the front of his sweep, his heart wrenched by the sailor's tale. Of course, there was nothing the surfman could have done to prevent the wreck; it had happened too far out on the lake. Still, he felt guilty, as if it were his dream that had caused the shipwreck to happen.

THE DREAM

After a time, Ben stumbled upon the drowned body of a man, face down and partially buried by the sand. When Ben turned the body over, he saw the face of the well-dressed man from his nightmare. Ben dropped to his knees, gasping for breath as he realized that his dream *had* foretold the shipwreck. But who was the man? Reluctantly, he forced himself to search the dead body, seeking the man's identity. Finding a pocket watch, Ben opened it and read the inscription. It belonged to Captain Peter Minch, owner of the *Western Reserve*.

27

The Rescuer

UPPER PENINSULA

My buddies and I—my name is Grant—take an annual hunting trip to the Upper Peninsula once a year. We haven't missed a year since our teens, and we don't intend to. Gene, Jake, and I take great pride in our ability to stalk game through woods and swamps and meadows. We had become skilled trackers in the process, and it never bothered anyone if one of us lagged behind, because we knew he could quickly catch up. But to be safe, we had a strict policy in place. If one of us remained missing for more than a half hour, the others would backtrack until they found him, just in case something unexpected had happened. I was the one most guilty of lagging behind. I was a closet naturalist and took more delight in examining the flora than in hunting the fauna.

Our most recent trip was in midsummer. On the last day, we woke to a gloriously sunny, warm morning. We left camp early, as Gene and Jake were intent on going home with something large and four-footed if it meant creating the creature out of sticks and swamp grass!

I walked at a slower pace than the others, letting them pull ahead while I leisurely enjoyed the woods and the glimpses I caught of birds and little creatures going about their business. When I reached a swampy area, I slowed down even more, taking great care as I picked my way through the grass and the marshy spots.

All at once, I glimpsed a mammoth-sized turtle out toward the center of the wetland. I moved forward to get a better look. And that's when I got myself into trouble. I leapt lightly onto what I supposed to be a dry patch of mud, but I found out quickly that there was nothing dry about it. In no time flat I was up to my armpits in mud and sinking. I flung both arms out instinctively to help keep my head above the surface, and I felt my rifle slide out of my grasp. It disappeared with a plopping sound to lord-knows-where beneath the slime.

I gave a loud shout for help, hoping Gene and Jake weren't too far ahead to hear me. The effort pushed me farther down into the mud, and my arms started sinking along with the rest of me. I had no idea how deep this mud was, but I figured if I kept on sinking, I was a goner. I shouted again, not quite so enthusiastically, and felt myself slip down another few inches.

I decided to remain very calm and still. I was stuck fast, and there was nothing solid within reach. My only hope was that the mud did not go deep enough to cover my face. I strained my ears hopefully, listening for answering shouts from my friends and the sound of running feet. But not a sound reached my ears, save for the whistles and chirps of birds happily flitting through the forest.

My heart was pounding ferociously as I slowly continued to sink into the thick, vile-smelling mud of the swamp. Before long, only my shoulders, neck, and head remained above the muck. I yelled again, my voice shrill with fear, and I felt myself sink a little farther once again. Through my mind flashed the face of my pretty young wife, pregnant with our first child. It was going to be a boy, and we'd been so happy painting his room and buying baby furniture the weekend before my trip. Only a week ago, but suddenly it felt like a lifetime. What would happen to Sarah and my boy if I died?

Suddenly, the overwhelming smell of rotten garbage filled the air, piercing through the stink of the mud. I heard the soft thud of footsteps and looked up, my heart pounding with hope. A huge, shaggy figure emerged from the trees beside the quagmire and stopped to peer down at me. It looked sort of like an ape, with a hairy body, long arms, and a flat brown face. Its eyes were round and dark, its ears small, and its nose flat. It had big hands and even bigger feet. Undoubtedly, it was a yeti. I'd heard of these creatures all my life—they're the "Bigfoot" of the north country—but I had never believed they really existed until now.

The yeti took in my predicament at a single glance. It turned its huge body and snapped off a long, sturdy branch from a nearby tree. A moment later the leafy end landed beside my face in the mud, and I gasped with relief and struggled desperately against the suck of the mud to free a hand. My right arm came loose with an ugly slurping sound, and I grasped the proffered branch. In another moment my left hand was out and I was clinging to the branch for dear life as I sank so low my chin was nearly covered with mud.

I kept my mouth firmly sealed, breathing hard through my nose as the yeti started pulling back on the branch, hand over massive hand. It was a fierce struggle. The mud didn't want to let me go. A couple of times I screamed in pain, feeling as if I were being ripped in half by opposing forces. The yeti seemed to understand the problem, because he slowed down and began to ease the branch forward just a little at a time. Inch by slow inch I emerged from the mire, until suddenly the mud released me with a sharp, watery popping sound. I flew the last few feet and fell on top of my rescuer, who had toppled to the ground when the pressure of the mud released so suddenly.

For a timeless moment I stared into the brown face and dark eyes of the yeti, my nose taking in the musty, sour smell of its fur. My six-foot frame seemed childlike compared with his, and I was suddenly reminded of my huge father, who gave me bear hugs every night when I was a toddler. Then the strangeness of the encounter and the thousands of differences that separated our two species intruded, and we rolled away from each other, springing to our feet several yards apart.

"Th . . . thank you," I gasped.

To my astonishment, the creature nodded in acknowledgment. I wondered if it understood English. My whole body was trembling with stress and adrenaline. I wanted to flee from this strange being, and yet I wanted the moment to go on forever. But just as suddenly as it appeared, the yeti retreated into the woods, leaving me shivering and shaking on solid ground.

It was then that I heard my friends shouting my name. The half-hour-apart rule had been exceeded and they had come looking for me—just a smidgen too late to pull me out of the mud. If the yeti hadn't happened by, there would have been nothing left of me for them to find.

THE RESCUER

Moments later, Gene and Jake were exclaiming in horror at my muddy appearance and bare feet. My boots were lost forever in the swamp mud, along with my rifle. But I didn't care—I was blessedly alive, and that's all that mattered. I was burning to tell them about the yeti, but I was afraid they would laugh. Instead, I told them I had pulled myself out of the mud by tugging on the low-lying branches of a nearby tree.

My friends were too agitated to notice that there was no tree within reach of the churned-up area where I had lain. Soon there would be nothing for them to see, no way for them to tell where I had fallen into the mud. The swampy spot was rapidly returning to its normal pristine state, having already swallowed half of the yeti's tree branch. I shuddered, reminded of how narrow my escape had been.

I winced my way back to camp in my bare, muddy feet, thankful for each stubbed toe and scraped ankle—each a welcome reminder that I was alive. After cleaning myself off and having a hot meal, I felt much better. I still didn't tell my friends about the yeti, though I rather thought that I would tell my wife. Sarah was also a closet naturalist, and she would have no trouble believing my story.

I got up before sunrise the next morning—the day we were to leave—and hiked back to the spot where I had almost perished. Removing my gold class ring, I placed it on a large rock, thinking that it might fit the smallest finger on the yeti's hand. I looked around in the growing daylight, but saw nothing. Still, I called out: "Please take this gift, with my thanks."

I was partway down the trail when some instinct made me look back over my shoulder. I saw the yeti standing beside the rock, gazing at the ring, which gleamed in the rays of the rising sun. It reached out a huge hand and picked up the glittering gold object, just as the sun came blazing over the horizon. I blinked my eyes against the sudden glare. When my sight cleared, the yeti was gone.

I smiled to myself and walked back the way I had come, toward camp, the road, and home.

28

The Devil's Coach

GROSSE POINTE WOODS

Now Jacques L'Esperance had an extremely good eye for horseflesh, as everyone in Grosse Pointe knew, so it was not surprising that he had the best stable in the territory. But he outdid himself the day he brought home a massive matched pair of black horses upon his return from a journey to Chicago.

No one had ever seen the like of them. They were hands taller than the average work horse and could pull the heaviest carriage with ease. Yet they were as sleek and slender as thoroughbreds and just as fast. At full gallop, it looked as if the horses' hooves didn't touch the ground. People called them "Jacques' flying horses," and the two blacks became famous throughout the territory. Folks lined the streets to gaze at them whenever Jacques rode out in his carriage.

Jacques was mighty proud of those horses, and he gave the greatest attention to their care. No one else was allowed to tend them, and he would rather have sold his soul to the Devil than sell his blacks.

Folks far and wide wanted to know where Jacques bought the horses and if any more were available. To each who inquired, Jacques told the same story. On his way home from Chicago one afternoon, he'd met a funny little man with a twisted, wry face wearing a brown tunic and a peaked green cap. The little man was tending to the massive black horses by the side of the road, and he was hopping mad because his master had left him behind with the mighty steeds, both of whom were winded and foaming at the mouth from heavy travel. The twisted little man had offered to sell Jacques the horses for an astonishingly low price, and the stable owner had been quick to take him up on his proposition. Money changed hands, and Jacques led the tired horses away to a beautiful clearing near a stream. He washed and curried them tenderly while they cropped the sweet grass and drank the cold water and recovered nicely from their ordeal. The little man had vanished as soon as the money was in his hand, and he did not reappear.

Jacques had been home with his new horses for about a month when an unexpected knock came on his door. There stood the twisted little man in his brown tunic and his peaked green cap. His master had sent him for the horses, the little man said. Jacques was annoyed. He had paid for the horses fair and square, and he told the little man so in no uncertain terms. The tiny man offered to return Jacques' money with an extra bonus for the inconvenience, but Jacques would have none of it. He had a perfect breeding pair of the finest horses ever seen in the territory, and he would not part with them for either love or money.

The twisted little man grew angry, but there was nothing he could do to reclaim the horses, for the law was on Jacques' side. The little man stomped and cursed and jumped up and down until Jacques was forced to threaten him with a rifle to get him to leave the property. Uncomfortable and worried, Jacques set up a special guard to watch the house and stables that night, and for many nights following. But the little man did not return, and eventually, Jacques relaxed his vigil.

Early one morning two months later, Jacques tromped through the deep, newly fallen snow to the stables to see how the horses had fared during the cold blizzard that had blanketed the country the previous night. To his shock, he found the pair quivering with fatigue and dripping with foam. They were in almost the same condition as when he had first seen them at the side of the road to Chicago.

Speaking to the horses gently, he checked them over for injuries and found many bloody lash marks upon their backs. Jacques was both infuriated and puzzled. There was no way anyone could have taken the horses out during that terrible storm, and yet it was obvious that someone had.

Jacques ministered carefully to his beloved horses, rubbing them down until they were calm and quiet, their breathing normal. He slathered ointment on their wounds, made sure there was no swelling or bruising on their slender legs, then blanketed them gently. All the while he was thinking furiously. This was the work of the twisted little man. He knew it in his bones. But how had he done it? And why had he returned the pair after stealing them?

Jacques slept in the barn that night, keeping one ear open for the return of the sprite. All was silent until the stroke of midnight. Then Jacques heard the rattle of a harness and a thump in the cleared-out yard before the barn doors. In walked the twisted little man, and he opened the stall doors and led the two blacks out front. Jacques crept along behind, keeping to the shadows.

When Jacques reached the doorway, he gasped aloud in shock and then clapped a hand over his mouth to muffle the sound. An ornate black coach hovered a foot above the ground. Attached to it were four mighty horses, the brothers and sisters of his matched pair. Two empty traces indicated where his horses belonged.

As Jacques watched, the twisted little man led the horses up into the air and strapped them into the harness with the other four. While the tiny imp was busy, Jacques slipped into the empty coach and hid himself behind the black curtains. A moment later, he heard the imp crawl up on the box and crack his whip. A great, howling whirlwind swirled around the coach, blowing the snow every which way. The horses moved forward, straining within the massive harness and stretching their mighty legs. The coach gave an uneven lurch and then began to rise as the black horses stepped out upon the mighty wind, running upon it as if it were solid ground. The coach rose high into the air and flew off into the night sky.

Jacques peered in wonder out the window and saw the moonlit snowscape below him. He had never dreamed the countryside would look so beautiful from above. Then he saw a huge blackness split open the sky. It resembled the yawning mouth of a predator, and its darkness blotted out the stars and cast shadows over the moon. The imp was aiming the coach right at the darkness. Jacques shuddered and pulled the curtains tightly around him. He did not want anything living in that darkness to see him.

A moment later, they were through the dark doorway and the coach settled down upon the ground. They were bowling along through a dim landscape that seemed permanently stuck

THE DEVIL'S COACH

in twilight. There were dark trees and bushes, dusky brown roads, and a lowering gray sky, but there seemed to be no true light anywhere. And to Jacques' horror, he found he could hear the sound of agonized screams and terrified sobbing carried on the wind, as if the land itself wept in despair.

He did not know how long they traveled through this dark country. It could have been moments or years. Finally, in front of the coach, a terrible red glow appeared on the horizon. It grew brighter and brighter, making strange shadows appear and disappear among the gray bushes and trees that crowded against the edge of the road.

Suddenly, the coach burst into an open area on the edge of a vast expanse. Down at the bottom raged a huge, burning lake made of fire and brimstone and lava, which writhed and seethed and flung great red arms up into the air.

Jacques expected them to turn and follow a lane along the side of the cliff, but the horses kept going straight toward the edge. He bit down on a scream as they flung themselves off the cliff. At once, the mighty whirlwind returned to catch the coach and brace the hooves of the black horses as they ran down through the empty air toward the lake of fire at the base of the cliff.

Jacques clung desperately to the side of the coach as they plummeted down and down. He was afraid he would fall out and plunge headfirst into the terrible lake of molten lava that burned and churned below them. The air was so hot that it steamed around him, and his hair started to sizzle. The red light was dazzling his eyes, and so at first he did not see the black island at the center of the lake or the black castle that stood upon it.

The horses pulled up sharply a hundred feet above the rolling lake of fire and ran straight toward the dark palace. The coach came to a halt in a grand black courtyard at the base of a wide, two-story staircase leading to the palace doors. The courtyard glowed with a dim, dark light.

As soon as the coach slowed, Jacques tumbled out and leapt under a stone bench beside the staircase, terrified of what would happen if the master of this terrible dark country found him inside the coach. The air in the courtyard was cool and pleasant—a strange contrast to the terrible seething fire just outside of the black palace. Jacques shivered and hugged himself tightly against the chill as a sharp tenor voice rang out from the door of the palace.

"Lix Tetrax," the voice cried. At once, the imp on top of the coach straightened up and turned to face the massive doorway at the top of the grand staircase.

"Master!" he said.

Jacques could not see the wide palace staircase, which climbed two stories to the left of the bench under which he cowered. But he could hear footsteps clicking on the stone as someone—the Master—descended.

"I see you have returned my horses," the Master said coldly. "They are back for good, I presume?"

From his concealed position, Jacques could just make out the sheepish look on the imp's face. "Well, no," Lix Tetrax said. "I told your lordship that the man wouldn't sell them back to me. What can I do? He's a baptized soul and a pious one to boot! The only reason I can get near the horses at all is because the farm itself hasn't been blessed by a priest, and even then it was terribly hard to call up the wind I needed to raise and land the coach."

"Lix Tetrax," the Master said, "you are whining."

A pair of beautifully polished shoes in the very latest style appeared on the bottom step beside Jacques' bench.

"Master," Lix Tetrax pleaded, "the best I can do is to borrow the horses at night. And even that's risky. If that man ever found out what I was doing, he'd have them blessed lickety-split and they'd be lost to us forever."

Jacques was now staring at beautifully tailored black trousers and the bottom half of an immaculately cut black coat. He had expected to see hooves and a long red tail, but the master of this place had apparently preferred to take on the appearance of a man instead of a demon.

"They were almost lost to us forever when you sold them to a Christian man out of spite," the Master said. "I want you to get them back. Offer the man whatever he desires! Just get me back my horses!"

"I tried . . ." Lix Tetrax began.

"Get them back," the Master howled in rage. Around them, the lights went out completely, while outside the palace the lake of fire gave a mighty roar and rose higher and higher until it almost eclipsed the walls of the black palace.

Lix Tetrax (and Jacques under his bench) cowered in terror.

"Yes, Master," the imp babbled. "I will get them back."

At once, the raging fires subsided and the black light sprang up in the courtyard once again. The imp hurriedly jumped down and opened the coach door for the Master. As soon as the imp climbed back up on the box, Jacques slipped out from under the stone bench and slid into the empty luggage rack at the back of the coach. There was no way he was going to be left behind in this dark place.

The swirling wind rose, the six black horses strained in their harness, and then the coach was flying up and up, out over the lake of fire and into the dim countryside above.

Jacques never forgot that night's journey. The Master had his finger in many pies, both in the human world and the netherworld. The coach swept back and forth between the dark country and the land above, the master in turn visiting a coven of witches, supervising the activities of the lesser demons, calling up a terrible life-taking storm at sea, and whispering darkness into the ears of a young king. Just before dawn, Lix Tetrax called up one final wind to drop the Master back at his dark palace in the middle of the lake of fire. Then the imp drove the coach through the netherworld, out the gaping mouth of darkness, and down to Jacques' farm.

Jacques tumbled into a deep drift of snow beside the barn and lay there until his horses were back inside and the black coach had departed. Then he leapt to his feet and ran down the icy road toward the church at the center of town. He was not leaving his farm or his horses unblessed for one minute longer than he had to.

Much to his surprise, not only did his priest believe Jacques' story, but he came right out to the farm with a bottle of holy water, still clothed in his dressing gown. The priest blessed Jacques and his wife and his sons. He blessed the house and the frozen fields and the barn. He blessed all the creatures on the farm, and drew crosses of holy water upon the brows of each horse in the barn.

When the priest drew near the black horses, however, they began to stomp uneasily and shy away. Jacques and his sons had to hold them down while the priest prayed over them. The horses screamed as if in agony when the holy water touched them, and Jacques and his sons watched in amazement as the holy water steamed off their hides in one mighty gust. When the steam dissipated, the forehead of each horse was branded with a shiny black cross. As soon as the holy brand appeared between their eyes, all the fight went out of the blacks. They settled down immediately and began pulling at the hay in their racks.

Jacques and his sons fervently thanked the priest. They rubbed down the horses, wrapped them carefully in their winter blankets, and together walked out of the barn and started down the slippery track to the farmhouse, where Jacques' wife was preparing a hearty breakfast.

As Jacques, his sons, and the priest turned into the snow-encrusted lane, they saw a small, twisted man approaching the house, coming down the road that led from the woods beyond the farm. When he reached the boundary of Jacques' property, the tiny imp came to an abrupt stop—as if he had smacked into an invisible wall—and fell backward with a curse. The men watched as he leapt up and ran forward again, hands outstretched. His gnarled palms smashed into the invisible wall of holiness once more, and the imp let out a stream of curses so vile that the priest clapped his hands over his ears to shut them out.

"What am I going to tell the Master?" Lix Tetrax howled, stomping up and down in fury. "What am I going to tell the Master?"

The last few words echoed strangely, as if they were shouted from within the depths of a fathomless cavern rather than out in the open. The sprite's voice grew louder and louder, and in it Jacques heard once more the screams of the damned that had haunted the edge of the wind in that dark, dark country where his two black horses had first resided.

Then a howling wind rose up around the twisted little man, forming into a massive tornado that stretched into the sky. It whipped the trees and the snow into a blinding column of ice with the imp at its center. But the air surrounding the farm was protected by the priest's blessing, and remained still and calm. Once, twice, three times the tornado of ice and snow bounced off the protective wall around Jacques' property. Then it vanished.

The priest took a deep breath and crossed himself. Beside him, Jacques' sons trembled with fear. Jacques, having seen much worse the night before, patted the priest on the back, gave his sons a reassuring look, and led them all to the farmhouse for breakfast. Then Jacques hitched up his blessed black horses to his carriage and drove the priest back to the church along the now-empty road, which showed no sign of the devilish tornado that the imp had conjured up just an hour before.

As he helped the priest down from the carriage, the old man took Jacques' hand. "My son," the priest said, "I will pray that the demon and his Master will leave you and your family alone."

"I would appreciate that, Father," Jacques said.

The priest's prayer must have worked, for Jacques never saw the imp again, and his horses remained with him until they died of old age many years later. But the good folk of Grosse Pointe still bless their houses and their creatures with holy water to keep the Devil and his minions away, just in case.

29

The Coffin of Snakes

L'ANSE

Some folks said it was a magic spell that did it. Others thought it was because of a too-pious upbringing. Whatever the case, it caused a terrible scandal in the town of L'Anse when Julienne, daughter of the God-fearing farmer Dubois, went to live with that blackguard Lizon without benefit of marriage. Lizon was a swarthy, dark-haired wretch who had appeared one day from who-knows-where and opened a tavern that quickly became the haunt of the most disagreeable and vile men in the region.

Lizon was an avowed atheist who did not hold with religion, and he was against marriage because it was sanctioned by the church. He represented everything that the local priest preached against; yet from the moment he set foot in town, the beautiful, God-fearing Julienne Dubois was fascinated with him. Much to Farmer Dubois' chagrin, the tavern owner was equally taken with her, and courted her openly. Somehow, Lizon persuaded the gentle, church-going Julienne to come away with him without benefit of a clergyman's blessing.

One evening, Farmer Dubois came home to an empty house with nary a note to explain his daughter's vacant room. But he knew where she had gone, and his heart just about broke with the pain of her departure.

The news of the scandal was everywhere by the next morning. The village priest was appalled by yet another demonstration of the evil forces that were gaining power in his parish. No matter how hard he prayed, how sternly he preached, or how much he canvassed and cajoled, the people of his parish seemed to be turning away from the teachings of God to follow the dark paths blazoned by Lizon. As the months passed from summer to autumn, the number of churchgoers dwindled and the number of taverngoers increased.

Then one Sunday in late fall, the doors of the church burst open in the middle of the priest's sermon. Julienne Dubois stumbled up the aisle and threw herself on her knees before the altar. She was dazed and exhausted, as if she had just awoken from a fevered dream, and she begged the priest and the good people of the church to forgive her for her sins.

So great was her emotion that Julienne could not utter a word to her father when she saw him. She just held out her hands pleadingly as tears rolled down her thin, white cheeks. Farmer Dubois tottered from his pew, almost as shaken as his daughter. He gathered the girl up in his arms, praising God for the miracle that had returned her to him. Dubois took Julienne home immediately and put her to bed. The priest and the doctor both came, one to pray with her and one to prescribe a tonic to restore her to health and well-being.

In spite of Julienne's miraculous return to the church, attendance continued to dwindle. The heart of the good priest often knew despair when he heard the compelling but foul stories emanating from the tavern. Word of terrible gatherings and magic spells began sweeping through the town, fascinating many of the younger people. As the holy Christmas season approached, the priest lost all hope and began to prepare for the closing of the church at the end of the holy days.

On Christmas Eve, a band of young men began dancing through the streets. They performed odd but amusing mummer's plays, sang Christmas songs, and asked families to donate meat to feed the less fortunate. Pleased by this show of goodwill, the faithful opened their doors to the masked dancers, including Farmer Dubois, who was hosting a small Christmas service in his home. It was not until a terrible scream came from the rear of the house that anyone realized that the performers had not come to celebrate goodwill to all; quite the reverse, in fact. While those gathered in the house had been listening to the mummers' songs, Lizon had climbed in through a side window and carried Julienne away with him.

Fighting their way free of the masked dancers, Dubois and his friends pursued the tavern owner back to his taproom. They found Julienne broken and bleeding in a back room. She rocked back and forth, babbling nonsense words and sobbing, her sanity gone. The men ran Lizon to ground in the taproom, but the tavern owner and his mummers kept them at bay with loaded rifles.

Thus was the scene when the priest arrived at the tavern. Standing framed in the darkened doorway, the priest pointed a finger at Lizon and pronounced judgment upon him. From that day forth, Lizon was excommunicated from the church. Because he was a plague to the people and an enemy of the church, his soul would never rest in the grave. Because so many of the people in the town had followed him into evil, the very church building that the townsfolk had abandoned would fall into ruin and be utterly destroyed.

An ominous silence followed the priest's curse. One by one, the masked mummers put down their weapons and disappeared into the dark night, fearing that the priest's curse would follow them if they remained at Lizon's side. But Lizon stood proud and defiant, unafraid of the priest's dark words. Holding his rifle trained on the priest, he spewed forth obscenities and blasphemy of the worst sort. He was still shouting when a group of men closed in on him, removed his weapon, and threw him into prison.

The priest packed his belongs that very night and left the town of L'Anse to its fate. At the moment of his departure, darkness swept over the town, and with it came sickness and violence and despair. Thunderclouds rolled in and did not move. All week long, the rain fell heavy and hard. Lizon was hung from the neck in the rain the day after New Year's. The wind whistled shrilly around the gallows as fog—in the shape of grim, faceless men—streamed into the town, sending people running for their homes.

The brave few who remained in the square cut Lizon's body down and threw it into a rough wooden coffin. A grave was hacked out of the ground near the tavern, and the casket was lowered into its depths. As the casket hit the bottom of the pit, a fierce hissing sound filled the air, and the lid of the coffin began to swell. Suddenly, it burst open and a writhing swarm of large gray snakes with beady black eyes and flicking forked tongues came pouring out. The gravediggers screamed and ran in all directions as the snakes bubbled forth from the coffin and slithered their way out of the pit. At the same moment, a roaring

THE COFFIN OF SNAKES

crash came from near the lake. The church, its foundations undermined by the constant lash of waves during the stormy week, had collapsed into the floodwaters, never to rise again.

The coffin was completely empty when the gravediggers finally returned to complete their grim task. But ever afterwards, the ground over Lizon's empty coffin would heave and sway during a storm as if it were disturbed by something bubbling up from underneath it, and sometimes a blue will-o'-the-wisp would dance over the place at night.

30

Sam Meets Death

KALAMAZOO

Sam Goodwin worked hard for a living, there's no doubt about that. He was a laborer on a local farm, and he spent every day from sunup to sundown tilling the fields and harvesting the crops, tending to the livestock and chasing away bears and other wild critters that had an eye on the chickens and the sheep. He was so plumb tired out at the end of each day that he had barely a word for his good wife Millie except "hello dear" and "please pass the stew."

Now, Millie didn't mind her husband's silence, since she knew he was tired from honest labor. But she was a mite annoyed by his good-night prayers. Just before bed, Sam would fall down on his knees and pray. "O Lord," he would plead, "please come take me out of this troublesome world." Millie would frown at him from the bed; she didn't like it when he talked about dying and leaving her alone. She thought he should be happy to have a good wife and a steady job and a nice house of his very own.

"You should be thanking the good Lord for his blessings, not begging him to take you away," Millie would scold. But Sam was a stubborn man, and he wouldn't change his nightly prayer.

After Sam went to work, Millie would often visit her neighbor Martha, and they would do laundry together or make soap or churn butter or piece a quilt. One day Millie told Martha all about Sam's nightly prayer and how much it annoyed her. Martha's husband Victor, who had come home for his lunch, laughed until he about split open his sides.

"That Sam," Victor said when he caught his breath, "what do you think he would do if the good Lord ever answered his prayer?"

"He'd head for the hills," Martha said with a grin.

"He'd hide under the bed," Millie corrected.

"I think we should find out which it is," Victor said, rubbing his hands with glee. The two ladies began to giggle at the thought, and the three conspirators put their heads together and made a plan to cure Sam of his desire to "depart this troublesome world."

When Sam got home that evening, Millie was cooking dinner and tending to their old cat Blackie, who was blind and nearly deaf. Sam scooped up his beloved pet and finished feeding the old cat her mush, which was the only food Blackie could swallow. Stroking the graying cat behind the ears, he asked Millie how her day had gone. Millie had a hard time keeping a straight face when she told him that she'd spent the day with Martha churning butter. She quickly changed the subject by inquiring about his work on the farm, and Sam told her of the day's events.

At bedtime, Millie donned her nightgown and wrapper. Then she carefully opened the window a smidge before sitting down before the mirror to braid her hair. Sam came into the room in his nightshirt, dropped to his knees beside the bed, and prayed loudly: "O Lord, please come take me out of this troublesome world."

Millie bit her lip and stared blindly into the mirror as a sepulchral voice from outside the window answered.

"Saaaaaam! Saaaaaaaam!" the voice moaned. Sam jumped and looked around.

"What was that?" he asked abruptly.

"What was what, dear?" asked Millie, hiding a smile. Victor was doing a splendid job, she thought, keeping her face blank as she turned toward her husband.

"Someone called my name!" Sam exclaimed.

"I didn't hear anything," Millie said, rising and walking over to the bed. "You must have imagined it. Come to bed now." She climbed into the bed and pulled the covers up to her chin.

"I did hear something," Sam said grumpily, but he obediently slid into bed beside her. He blew out the candle and settled down to sleep beside his wife.

"Saaaaaam! Saaaaaaam!" Victor's spooky voice wailed from outside the window.

Sam sat bolt upright. "There it is again," he exclaimed into the darkness.

"There is what again?" asked Millie, suppressing a smile with her hand.

"Someone is calling my name," Sam said.

"Don't be ridiculous," Millie said. "Who would be calling your name at this hour?"

From outside the window, the eerie voice wailed again: "Sam! Sam! This is Death calling to you. Answer me, Sam Goodwin!"

"Holy Moses! It's Death," Sam shouted. "Death is calling to me!"

"Death?" Millie exclaimed. But Sam hushed her. "I can't hear what Death's saying," he cried.

"Saaaam! Saaaaaaam! Your soul is required at the bar of God tonight," Victor wailed from outside the window.

The words rang loud and clear through the room. When he heard them, Sam started shaking so badly that the bed rattled.

"Well, if Death is calling to you, you'd better answer him," Millie said briskly. But Sam was no longer beside her.

"Sam?" she called. "Sam, where are you?"

"I'm here," Sam's voice said from underneath the bed.

Millie was startled. "Sam Goodwin, what are you doing under the bed?" she demanded.

"I'm hiding from Death," Sam said sheepishly, as Victor wailed his name again from outside the window.

Millie could hear the floorboards creaking as Sam shifted his weight. "Do me a favor, Millie, and tell Death that I left on a trip three days ago and you don't know when I'll get back."

"I will do no such thing!" Millie snapped. "You've been begging the good Lord to take you out of this troublesome world, and now he's answered your prayer. You come out from under that bed this instant and go with Death just like you've been praying all these years."

There came a deep sigh from underneath the bed and a prolonged wail from outside the window. "I knew you'd say that," Sam said, crawling out from under the bed into the darkened room. "Give me a kiss then, and I'll be off."

Millie gave him a kiss and walked him down to the front door. Sam was shaking so much that he could hardly walk, and

Millie could barely suppress her giggles. This trick would cure him of praying for Death, she was sure of it.

Sam opened the front door, and a blast of frigid air swept in from outside. Millie shivered, surprised by the coldness on what should have been a balmy summer night. Outside on the lawn, a huge figure in a white sheet came toward them, arms lifted dramatically above its head. "Saaaaaaam!" Victor wailed, flailing his arms wildly.

But Sam looked beyond the ghostly form, toward the small gate in the picket fence that surrounded their yard. A look of terror crossed Sam's face. He gasped aloud and clutched his heart as the color drained from his cheeks. Confused, Millie and the sheet-draped figure turned to gaze at the fence.

Standing just inside the gate was a hooded form, blacker than the blackest shadow. Two white-blue eyes blazed out of the cowl that covered its head, and skeletal fingers gripped a large scythe. The air around the figure seemed to crackle with the energy of a thousand bolts of lightning, its robes whipped in an unseen wind, and its skeletal feet were half-buried in swirling gray clouds that stretched back and back into eternity.

Millie's heart started pounding so hard that it nearly burst from her chest. She gasped in horror and clutched Sam's shoulder as the figure slowly raised an arm and pointed a skeletal finger at them.

"No," Millie shouted. "You can't have him."

"*Come away from this troublesome world*," the figure intoned in a voice like a funeral bell.

From underneath the white sheet, Victor gave a terrified shriek and bolted across the lawn toward his house.

"*Come away from this troublesome world*," Death intoned. The eldritch voice echoed and reechoed through Millie's bones. She gripped Sam's shoulder still harder.

"You can't have my Sam," Millie said. She swallowed hard. "Take me instead."

Sam came out of his daze when he heard her words. "No!" he shouted. "No, Millie. I'm the one who prayed for this. I'll go."

"*Come away from this troublesome world*," Death intoned for a third time.

Millie clung tightly to Sam, glaring at the glowing black figure by the gate. "I won't let you go," she said to Sam.

From the porch near their feet came a sudden soft meow. Sam and Millie looked down and saw the glowing spirit form of their old cat, Blackie. She was stretching, first her front legs, then her back. Finally, she gave an excited trill and hurried down the steps toward the dark figure by the gate. The glowing form of the little cat rubbed against Death's skeletal legs, and then leapt up into its arms. She meowed again, and then started to purr.

For a long moment, Millie and Sam stared deeply into the glowing eyes of Death. Then the dark figure by the gate vanished, and warmth flowed again into the summer night.

Millie and Sam collapsed against one another, trembling and gasping for breath. "Oh, Sam. Oh, Sam," was all Millie could say.

Finally Sam straightened up. "Was that Victor under the sheet?" he asked.

"Yes," Millie said, and she told him about the joke she had planned with the help of her neighbors. "I just wanted to get

SAM MEETS DEATH

you to stop saying that prayer," she cried. "I didn't mean to attract Death itself."

"I'm not so sure you did," Sam said, hugging her tightly. "After all, I was the one who made that prayer every night. Perhaps the good Lord sent Death to teach me a lesson about appreciating the fine things he has given me in this life. Or perhaps Death was already coming to our home to fetch Blackie."

As he spoke, Sam led his wife gently into the house and back up the stairs to their room. "Whatever the reason for Death's visit, you see before you a changed man," Sam concluded. "From now on, Millie, I'm going to thank God for my blessings and pray for a long and happy life each night before I go to bed. Starting right now."

And Sam Goodwin dropped down on his knees and loudly gave thanks for his many, many blessings, right then and there.

31

Estrid

DETROIT

"Estrid. Her name is Estrid!"

Gregory shouted the words aloud to the sleeping city. He hugged himself in glee and waltzed along the cobblestone road until he reached his small room at the back of the exclusive inn where he worked as a journeyman chef.

Gregory had just achieved journeyman status, and it came with an increase in salary. He was delighted, for now he could take a wife and begin his family. And Estrid was the lucky woman who would make him the happiest of men. The young chef chortled merrily and kicked his heels in a spasm of sheer delight. Maybe he was a bit of a fool to have fallen in love with a girl he'd never met, but Gregory didn't care. Time would take care of that problem.

Gregory had been making blood sausage for a gathering at the inn when he'd seen Estrid for the first time. He was mixing pig blood into the bowl with the other ingredients when a red flash outside the window caught his eye. Gregory looked outside and saw a woman walking down the lantern-lit cobblestone street. Her knee-length red hair swirled around her like a cloak. The woman's form was dainty and well-rounded in all the right places. Gregory could not see her face, but anyone with such gorgeous red hair must be beautiful. He couldn't take his eyes off the woman's hair.

Gregory watched until the woman disappeared around a corner. Only then did he realize he'd spilled most of the pig blood on the floor.

From that moment, Gregory longed to meet the red-haired woman, but night followed long night without a glimpse of her—until tonight. Gregory had been making blood pudding for tomorrow's special luncheon when he glimpsed the red-haired woman walking down the street in the light of the gas lamps. He put the pudding in the cold room, hands shaking with nerves, and bolted outside. To his relief, the woman was just turning the corner ahead of him. Gregory followed, calling, "Lady, please wait!" But she didn't hear him. She stayed a block ahead of him, moving swiftly through the twists and turns of the old city. Gregory's heart was thundering from so much unexpected exercise, and he was clutching a stitch in his side by the time the red-haired woman stopped suddenly before a door, turned a key in the lock, and slipped inside. He hobbled up the steps and knocked. After a moment, a lovely female voice called to him through the door, "Who is it?"

"It is I, Gregory, the journeyman chef from the inn," he called through the door. "Lovely lady, I have seen you passing the inn and I wish to court you. I make a fine salary and would be a very good husband. Lady, may I meet you?"

To his delight, the woman replied, "I have seen you at the inn, Gregory the chef, and I would like to meet you. But I cannot come out this evening. My parents are ill. Could you return tomorrow?"

Gregory shivered in delight. "I could come tomorrow. But lovely lady, at least tell me your name!"

Through the door, the woman cooed, "Estrid. My name is Estrid."

That night, Gregory dreamed of his new love. He saw Estrid walking away from him down the road that led to the woods outside town. Her blood-red hair floated around her like a cloak, gleaming in the starlight. He followed her, longing to see her lovely face, but she was always just a few yards ahead of him, following a winding path toward a dark cottage surrounded by tall pines. And then the morning sunlight woke him, and it was time to go to work.

Gregory hummed to himself as he worked. The usually temperamental journeyman actually joked with the kitchen boys, and he didn't even scold the server when he dropped a plate of salmon on the floor. The staff was amazed by the chef's good humor. But Gregory's mind wasn't on his work. He kept seeing Estrid's blood-red hair swaying around her as she walked home in the lamplight. He would see her tonight! How would he make it through the day?

The hours crawled slowly by, but at last Gregory was standing in his best suit, clutching a bouquet of blood-red roses. He raised his hand to knock, but before his knuckles brushed the wood, Estrid's voice spoke from behind the door.

"Gregory, I am sorry," she said. "My parents are still ill and I cannot go out with you tonight."

Gregory blinked in surprise. How had Estrid known he was here? But his surprise was swallowed swiftly by disappointment.

"I am sorry to hear they are ill," he said politely. "I have flowers for you. Will you open the door so I can give them to you in person?"

But Estrid said, "I hear my mother calling to me. I had better go to her. Would you leave the flowers by the door? And would you come tomorrow night instead, so we can meet?"

Her voice was so sweet and delicate that Gregory was smitten anew. He could wait one more night to meet his love. "Of course, my lady. I will see you tomorrow night."

"Good dreams, my Gregory," Estrid cooed through the door.

Gregory left the blood-red roses on the doorstep and floated home. "Estrid," he whispered to the wind. "Her name is Estrid." He tumbled into bed and dreamed at once of the lovely red-haired woman, always walking away from him down the cobblestone streets. All night long, he followed her through the twists and turns of the city and then out into the woods, down the dark path to the cottage in the pines. In his dream, he peered through a crack and saw Estrid with her back to him, stirring a pot of blood-red soup before the fire. It was the same color as her long, lovely red hair. *Turn around, Estrid,* Gregory willed. *Let me see your face.* But a sunbeam slanted through his window and woke him before Estrid finished stirring her soup.

Around noon, Gregory tossed the last of the tomato slices into the pot and put it over the fire to slowly simmer into a deep, thick tomato soup to be served with the supper that night. The blood-red soup looked so much like the soup he'd seen in his dream of Estrid that Gregory decided it must be a sign. She was making soup; he was making soup. They were meant for each

ESTRID

other! He sighed romantically and forgot to scold the kitchen boy for forgetting to fill the wood box.

Donning his best suit once again after the kitchen closed for the night, Gregory made his way through the twisted streets to Estrid's door. He knocked boldly, and Estrid answered at once, speaking through the door. "Gregory, my father is very poorly. You cannot come in."

Gregory's heart sank into his shoes. Estrid was avoiding him. She did not want to meet her clumsy suitor. As if she could read his mind, Estrid cooed, "Of course I must meet you, Gregory. I just cannot meet you now. But at midnight I will come to the fountain in the square beside the inn. Meet me there tonight, as I have met you in your dreams these last two evenings."

Gregory's eyes widened. "You sent me those dreams?"

"Of course," cooed the lovely voice. "You are my true love. I could not be with you in the flesh, so I came to you in your dreams."

A shiver ran down Gregory's spine. He was astonished at this sign of power from the delicate woman with the blood-red hair. And such a woman wanted him, a journeyman chef? It seemed like a miracle. "I will meet you by the fountain," he promised the lovely voice behind the door. And he danced all the way back to the inn, to the amused delight of all who passed him in the street.

Gregory spent the next two hours pacing back and forth in the square, waiting for Estrid to appear. Eventually, he tired of all the walking and sank down on a bench to wait. His eyes grew heavy as midnight approached. Gregory toppled slowly onto the seat of the bench and fell into a lovely dream. He was walking down the winding path through the woods toward the cottage. Firelight spilled through the partially opened door, and he could see Estrid bent over the steaming pot of blood-red soup, her red hair gleaming. As if she sensed his approach, Estrid called over her shoulder, "Come in, Gregory. I have been expecting you!"

All around the square, the world went silent and too still. Even the wind ceased batting the dead autumn leaves hither and thither across the cobbles. The gas lamps shivered behind their glass as a figure with flowing blood-red hair floated soundlessly down from the sky above the square and landed beside the sleeping Gregory. "Hello, love," Estrid cooed as her hair spilled across his prone form and writhed and wrapped itself around him. Each lock of hair sprouted slitted golden snake eyes and sank sharp fangs into the dreaming chef's neck to suck and suck his thick red blood.

In Gregory's dream, Estrid turned away from the fire at last to face her suitor. To his horror, the transfixed journeyman beheld the twisted, fanged visage of a hag. "I am happy to meet you," Estrid cooed.

Gregory screamed and tried to wake himself. But there was nothing to go back to. Every drop of blood had been drained from his sleeping body. In his last frantic moment of life, Gregory felt the dream Estrid wrap cloying arms around his soul. Then the hag opened her fanged mouth and bit down.

Eunice

JACKSON

Eunice and I became friends on our very first day of grammar school. We studied together and played games together and spent the night in each other's homes. Eunice's parents sent her to St. Mary's College in Indiana for upper school, but we remained best friends. Whenever she came home for holidays, we took up right where we left off, driving in the carriage together and giggling about beaus and attending the local sewing circle. Eunice's pa was one of the richest farmers in Michigan while my family was poor, but that didn't matter. Old Jacob was a bit ornery and tight-fisted, but he valued hard work, and I was a favorite. Indeed, I was very fond of the whole family and they of me. The old Crouch farmhouse was my second home.

I cried at Eunice's wedding and gave her a big hug, knowing that things would be different from then on. Eunice and her husband—who was a physician—would remain in her family home to take care of old Jacob, but I knew that Eunice's priorities had changed. There would no longer be time for the activities we had enjoyed when she was single. Still, I saw Eunice at church and around town, and we remained very fond of each other. In fact, I was the first non–family member with whom Eunice shared the news that she was expecting. We giggled excitedly and started planning right away.

That particular day I had some news of my own to share. I showed Eunice the sparkling ring on my finger, put there by a prosperous young farmer named Billy, whom I had been eyeing all through high school. It turned out that he—unbeknownst to me—had been eyeing me right back. Good thing his younger sister figured it out and started teasing her brother about me, or we'd have both been as old as Methuselah before he spoke up.

Eunice gave a loud cheer when she saw my ring and hugged me tight. "Our children will be best friends," she promised.

My betrothed and I planned to marry right after the harvest. Billy wanted to take me on a wedding trip to see his family back East before the heavy snows came. We would take the train all the way to New York! It was a terrible expense, but Billy claimed he'd been saving up for it since the day he first met me. Knowing Billy, this was probably true.

"I'll be round as a pumpkin by then," Eunice said with a smile. "But I will come to your wedding. Hopefully you will be back from your wedding trip before the baby arrives."

The rest of the visit was divided between discussing the baby, the wedding, and the Texas property old Jacob had bought a few years back. "Pa says it has turned out quite profitable," Eunice told me. "Pa always did have a good head for business. I told him we should plan to visit after the baby is born. They say Texas is quite warm in winter. It sounds heavenly compared to winter up here!"

"How right you are," I said. Michigan winters were all about snow, snow, and more snow.

True to her word, Eunice was round as a pumpkin when she came to my wedding, though dressed in the very latest Eastern style. She nearly eclipsed the bride in her finery, although, bless him, my Billy didn't even notice. He only had eyes for me in the handmade white gown my mama had sewn for me.

"It appears old Jacob's Texas holdings are pumping money into the Crouch household," my pa said later at the reception.

"I'm happy for Eunice," I said calmly. "She is a wonderful friend, and she adores her father. It couldn't happen to a nicer person."

Pa let it go. He was fond of Eunice, and old Jacob was a shrewd businessman who'd earned every penny of his money. Their hearts were in the right place, as evidenced by the more than generous wedding gifts quietly slipped into our new little house while Billy and I were still at the church.

Our wedding trip took longer than expected, but that didn't worry us. Between his parents and mine, we knew our snug little farm was well cared for while we gallivanted around the country. Eunice's baby would be more than a month old when we got back, and I was excited to learn if it was a boy or a girl.

Both families gathered at our small house to welcome us back. Everyone was merry, and the talk was light and focused on everything we had seen and done on our travels. But there was an underlying sadness to the occasion that I didn't understand. At one point I saw my pa pull Billy aside for a quiet word, but I never associated it with me until everyone had left and I brought two plates of my mother-in-law's superb apple pie to our comfortable chairs by the hearth.

"Your pa thought I was the one who should tell you the news," Billy began awkwardly, putting the plate of pie down on a side table.

"What news?" I asked, following suit with my own pie plate. Something in my husband's face told me the news was not good.

"Eunice, her husband, and her father were killed while we were away," Billy began.

I stiffened, and my eyes widened in shock. I sat numbly as Billy told me what happened. An intruder entered their household at night and shot old Jacob and Eunice's husband in the head. Eunice herself was shot five times. Her baby never had a chance to be born. Tracks were found in the snow and empty cartridges on the floor of the house. The servants had been arrested and then released from lack of evidence. The most common theory about the crime was that a large payment must have arrived from the Texas holdings and that the family had been killed for the money.

Somewhere during this recital, I started weeping and could not stop. I had known the whole family for years. Who could have done such a terrible thing? What kind of monster would shoot sweet, gentle Eunice, who was going to have a baby?

My husband took me to visit the graves the next day. Eunice was buried in St. John's Cemetery and old Jacob buried across town in the Crouch-Reynolds family cemetery, 5 miles away. It was a terrible moment for me, kneeling beside Eunice's gravestone to say good-bye to my friend and her unborn baby. I had sewn a little quilt for the child before we left on our wedding trip. I laid my gift on Eunice's tombstone and then wept in my husband's arms.

Just a few days after we returned from our wedding journey, Eunice's sister, Susan, was murdered by poison, shortly followed by one of Jacob's former farmhands. Last to die was Susan's husband. Investigations, accusations, and arrests were made. The whole town was in an uproar for months following the last murder. Several men went to trial, but no one was convicted of the crimes. The case remained open.

I was expecting my own first child by November of the following year. Snow was already on the ground and footing was uneven as I made my way into St. John's Cemetery around dusk with some hothouse flowers to place on Eunice's grave on the anniversary of her death. My husband wanted to come to the gravesite with me, but I preferred to be alone, so he remained on the road with the sleigh.

I stood for about five minutes in the cold, telling Eunice about the baby and our farm and the family gossip. All the things I would have told her if she were alive. Then I laid the flowers in front of the grave and stepped back toward the hard-trodden path through the snow.

Suddenly a light blazed behind me, brightening the twilight cemetery. I jumped in fright. I thought I was alone in the graveyard. Who had lit a lantern? I whirled, raising my hands, afraid the unknown murderer had returned. Then I saw a cloud of white light rising from the top of Eunice's tomb. It broke free from the stone and floated toward me. I ducked, instinctively covering my unborn child to protect it from the light.

The hazy cloud floated down the length of the cemetery and out onto the road, where it passed my dumbfound husband and spooked our horses. The horses took off in the opposite direction, dragging our sleigh behind them. By the time I navigated my way back along the slippery path to the road, Billy had regained control of the horses, turned the sleigh around, and was driving back to St. John's to pick me up.

"What is that thing?" he asked wide-eyed as he helped me into the sleigh. I felt his hand trembling in mine, and I suspected it was not just the exertion from stopping the horses that made him shake.

"I think it is Eunice's ghost," I replied, swallowing my own fear. "I want to see where she is going."

Billy nodded acquiescence. "We will need to keep the horses as far away as we can from that cloud of light or they will spook again" was his only reply.

We drove slowly down the road, following the hazy cloud. It was still glowing, but not as much as when it first rose from the grave. As we crossed town, I became convinced I knew where the cloud was taking us. When it turned into the Crouch-Reynolds cemetery, I knew for sure.

"Eunice is going to see old Jacob," I told my husband as he stopped the horses a good distance away from the hazy cloud of light. I left Billy with the sleigh and entered the second cemetery. Sure enough, the hazy cloud wafted over toward Jacob's tomb, where it hovered over the grave and brightened for a moment. Then it vanished into the stone.

In that instant, I heard the sound of Eunice's voice speaking, though I couldn't make out the words. She was answered by a

EUNICE

rumbling bass voice. It sounded like old Jacob. Then the light faded and I was alone in the cemetery.

I brushed away tears. Apparently, dead wasn't the same as gone. Eunice and old Jacob were together, somewhere beyond the grave. That's all I really needed to know.

I walked out of the cemetery and climbed into the sleigh beside my patiently waiting husband.

"Please take me home," I said. And he did.

33

The Lodger Returns

DETROIT

Kennette was quite the character here in Detroit. Everyone knew her. You never saw such a miser! She wore an old patched coat and begged food and fuel from her neighbors, even though she had plenty of money of her own. And she was about as rude as a body could be to everyone who spoke to her. To top it off, she was a skeptic. Sometime or another in her life, Kennette had read Voltaire and it stuck. She never went to church, didn't believe in the hereafter, and scoffed at anyone who was religious. I don't know why folks put up with her, but they did.

Kennette was not a nice person but, boy howdy, could she make a shoe. As a cobbler she was top notch. She charged a pretty penny for her shoes and boots, but they were worth it. I still have a pair made by Kennette, and they were worth the exorbitant price I paid. I've had them for more than a decade, and they still fit like a glove and look new.

The only time Kennette softened was when she played the fiddle. People passing in the street would stop and listen to Kennette whenever she took out her violin. Her music was heavenly, but I never told her so. The one time I mentioned heaven to Kennette, she spat on my new boots. And she had made 'em! So I just listened and enjoyed—from a distance.

Well, Kennette was getting on in years and couldn't work such long hours in her shop, so she decided to rent out one of her rooms to make some more money (and to get some supplemental use out of her boarder's fuel and food, but I digress). The lady to whom she rented the room was pious old Clarissa Jordan, who was a regular churchgoer and firmly believed in the hereafter. The whole neighborhood found it amusing to see such opposites sharing the same household.

Night after night, old Clarissa sat by the fireside, knitting and telling ghost stories to Kennette. The cynical cobbler scoffed at every one of them. "One day you'll see," Clarissa said each time Kennette jeered. It drove the cobbler crazy.

After the first tale, Kennette would growl and leap up from her chair, reaching for her fiddle. She could only stand one ghost story per night. Whenever Clarissa started a second, Kennette played the violin. Since Clarissa was an avid music lover, many of us speculated that this was the real reason she told so many ghost stories.

"And that's the tale of the *feu follet*," Clarissa concluded one winter evening over the click of her knitting needles. "That's the French name for it of course. We usually call it a will-o'-the-wisp or jack-o'-lantern. Did I ever tell you the story of the jack-o'-lantern?"

Kennette growled as usual, but on this particular night she did not reach for the violin. She'd had a bad day and was itching to take out her ire on someone. So she roared, "Fie on you, old woman! I do not believe in your stories. I don't believe in your heaven or your hell."

"And I *know* they exist," Clarissa said calmly, folding her knitting in her lap. The old lady's calmness infuriated the cobbler.

"Bah!" shouted Kennette. "Prove it, then. If you die first, you come back to this house and show me that there is an afterlife in which your soul still exists. If I die first and there is an afterlife, I will do the same. But I guarantee you that neither of us will come back!"

"Very well then," Clarissa said with a confident smile. "I will return, just as you request."

"Fiddlesticks!" Kennette snorted with rage, threw another log on the fire, and stomped off to bed.

Clarissa did not get out of bed the next morning. Kennette found her smiling sweetly in death, hands folded over her chest. For a moment the cobbler's wrinkled face softened with a hint of sorrow. Then she stomped off to call the undertaker to do his duties by the dead.

One evening about a week later, Kennette was discussing old Clarissa's funeral with a neighbor when a young lad who lived across the road paused to tell her that she'd left a light burning in her house. The miserly Kennette never left a light burning in the house, no matter how late she planned to be gone. The source of the light must be an intruder, come to rob Kennette.

The old cobbler rushed back to her house, only to find it dark and empty. Arming herself with the poker from the fireplace, she searched every room but found no sign of a thief. It made her nervous.

Kennette was careful to lock every door and window the next morning before leaving for the shop. Still, when she

THE LODGER RETURNS

returned home that night, her neighbors told her they'd seen a light glowing in her window just after dusk. Kennette went over every inch of the house again, but there was still no sign of an intruder and nothing had been taken.

Determined to get to the bottom of the mystery, Kennette left her shop the next afternoon, even though it meant losing half a day's wages, and snuck into her house through the back door so the intruder would not know she was home. She sat in her chair by the dark fireplace, shivering a bit in the cold, and waited with poker in hand as the sun slowly set. As the room darkened, Kennette pulled a shawl over her coat and glared at the front door. The intruder was costing her money. She would give the fellow what for as soon as he stepped inside her home.

Kennette waited and waited, getting colder and sleepier in the dark room. Finally, realizing the intruder was not going to make an appearance, she lit a small fire in the hearth, ate a frugal meal, and went to bed, still carrying the poker with her, just in case.

Kennette was half asleep when she saw a light coming upstairs, as if someone was ascending with a lantern. She sat up in bed, clutching the poker as the light drew nearer. Through the open doorway, she saw a phosphorescent white ball float over the top stair and down the hall toward her room.

Kennette's mouth dropped open in shock as the glowing light bounced jauntily over her threshold and stopped a few feet from her bed. Slowly the sparkling ball started to spin, growing larger until it took on the shape of Clarissa Jordan.

Kennette gave a yell of fright and dove beneath the covers, the poker still clutched in her hand. The glowing figure came closer. The light shone right through the blanket over her head.

Kennette swallowed and slowly peered out from under the bedclothes, right into the face of her former lodger.

"I know you," she gasped, trembling from head to toe. "Come no nearer."

Clarissa's shade stood still, watching Kennette with her head cocked questioningly.

Grudgingly, Kennette said, "You were right about the hereafter. I see that, now."

Clarissa Jordan smiled. "Did I ever tell you the story of the jack-o'-lantern?" she asked teasingly.

Kennette reared up and waved the poker at her former border. "Get away with you," she shouted. "No more ghost stories!"

Clarissa laughed and vanished.

The next day was Sunday. For the first time since she was a child, Kennette went to church. She brought her violin with her and played "Amazing Grace" for the offertory. It was Clarissa's favorite song.

Kennette never saw the ghost again. Apparently, one visitation was deemed enough to restore her childhood faith in the hereafter. Although it must be said, Kennette slept each night with a poker by her bed to discourage further ghostly communications, so that may have had something to do with it.

The Spinning Wheel

DETROIT

Fifty Masses. That was all she wanted.

On the day that Grand'-mère Duchene moved in with her youngest son and his wife, the first thing she said was: "When I die, I want you to buy fifty Masses for the repose of my soul." She wagged a bony finger under her son's nose. "Don't you forget, *mon cher* Henri. Fifty Masses for my soul."

"That's a lot of money, Grand'-mère," his wife, Marie, protested.

"Fifty Masses," Grand'-mère Duchene insisted, hobbling over to her spinning wheel. She took a seat and started the wheel spinning—*shhhooom, shhhooom, shhhooom.* "Don't you forget."

A stooped figure wearing a black shawl over her worn dress, Grand'-mère looked so frail that the least bit of wind might knock her down. But Henri knew his mother had a will of iron. He and Marie exchanged helpless glances. It was all they could do to keep food on the table for their five children. How could they afford to purchase fifty Masses for Grand'-mère Duchene when she passed?

Grand'-mère Duchene settled easily into the bustling household. She spent hours at the spinning wheel in the warm corner beside the fireplace. The family soon got used to the constant *shhhooom, shhhooom, shhhooom* of the whirling wheel. As she spun, Grand'-mère told the children all the old legends of French Canada or listened as they recited their lessons. The baby often sat near her feet, teething on a wooden doll or patting the newly spun thread. *Shhhooom, shhhooom, shhhooom.* For the children, the whirl of the spinning wheel was a happy sound—the sound of home.

Every morning when she sat down to spin, and every evening before she shuffled off to bed, Grand'-mère Duchene said to Henri: "When I die, I want you to buy fifty Masses for the repose of my soul."

"I hear you, *Maman.* You want me to buy fifty Masses," Henri replied, choosing his words with care so he would not make a promise he did not intend to keep. All he said was that he heard his mother, not that he would obey her.

Grand'-mère helped sew a lovely wedding dress for her eldest granddaughter, Josephine, made from the dainty white thread she had spun and Marie had woven into cloth for this special occasion. The pretty bride came to the warm corner by the fireplace and leaned over the spinning wheel, strangely silent for once, to kiss her grand'-mère goodbye before walking to the little house next door, which she would share with her brand-new husband.

"*Je t'aime,*" Josephine whispered, staring into the sunken dark eyes. A pang struck her heart. Grand'-mère looked so frail. Then, as she walked out the door, Josephine heard the spinning wheel start up—*shhhooom, shhhooom, shhhooom.* The bride relaxed. As long as the wheel kept spinning, all was well.

"Remember, fifty Masses for my soul," Grand'-mère called through the closing door. Josephine laughed happily. That Grand'-mère! Always going on about her fifty Masses.

Grand'-mère died in her sleep a week later. The children were heartbroken. It was autumn and snow would fly soon, so Grand'-mère was quickly laid to rest. Nothing was said to the priest about the fifty Masses Grand'-mère wanted purchased for her soul. Henri and Marie had spent more money than they could afford on the wedding, and they still had children to feed and owed money to the bank. Every penny was accounted for. There was none to spare for frivolities.

"Surely God has bypassed Purgatory for Grand'-mère. She was such a devout woman that He must have taken her straight to Heaven," Henri said to Marie. His wife nodded, rather uncertainly. It went against the grain to ignore Grand'-mère's wishes. Still, the money was needed elsewhere. Surely Grand'-mère would understand.

Henri felt guilty every time he saw the spinning wheel in the corner, so he bundled it up and put it in the attic. And that's when the trouble began. That night, after all the children were in bed, the house was suddenly filled with a low humming sound: *shhhooom, shhhooom, shhhooom*. As soon as he heard it, Henri bolted upright in bed. In the next room he heard his eldest son call, "Grand'-mère? Is that you?"

Shhhooom, shhhooom, shhhooom. The sound filled the house. Henri jumped up and lit a lantern with trembling hands. He rushed into the parlor and looked into the warm corner by the fireplace. It was empty. But the sound of spinning still filled the house: *shhhooom, shhhooom, shhhooom*.

When Marie touched his shoulder, Henri nearly jumped through the roof. She pointed toward the attic. *Shhhooom, shhhooom, shhhooom.* Yes, the sound was coming from upstairs. The hall was suddenly overflowing with excited children. "Grand'-mère is here! We want to see Grand'-mère," they exclaimed over and over.

"She is not here," Marie said firmly. "Grand'-mère is in heaven. You saw us bury her."

The children did not believe her. They could hear the spinning wheel whirling, and the only one who ever touched it was Grand'-mère. Therefore she must be here. They wouldn't go back to bed until they'd seen the empty corner for themselves. The two youngest children burst into tears when they realized Grand'-mère was not present. "But I can hear her spinning wheel," the baby wailed. "Where is she?"

Shhhooom, shhhooom, shhhooom. The sound of the spinning wheel reverberated through the parlor. The noise was getting louder.

"The sound is coming from the attic. Maybe she is up there," Henrietta, next oldest but one, said.

Henri and Marie exchanged glances. They did not want their children anywhere near the attic. Who knew what they would find up there.

Shhhooom, shhhooom, shhhooom. Pots and pans were rattling in the kitchen. The fireplace poker fell over, nearly hitting the baby on the head.

Before they could stop her, Henrietta ran barefoot down the hallway and wrenched open the door to the attic. Henri raced after her, followed by his wife and the whole brood. As soon as the attic door was open, the sound of spinning grew so loud it made their teeth vibrate.

SHHHOOOM. SHHHOOOM. SHHHOOOM.

Henrietta was climbing the ladder in the dark. Henri hastened after her with his lantern. But he did not need it. The attic was alight with an eerie phosphorescent glow. Henrietta stuck her head through the trap door and shrieked, "Grand'-mère! Grand'-mère!"

Henri flew up the ladder in a panic. When he reached the top, he saw his daughter hugging a stooped little figure in a black shawl who was sitting at the spinning wheel. Both Grand'-mère and her spinning wheel were the source of the blue-white light. The spinning wheel was turning so fast that it glowed red-hot.

As Henri staggered onto the attic floor, the ladder was overwhelmed with climbing children. In a moment, Grand'-mère was eclipsed by little arms hugging her fiercely while the ghostly spinning wheel kept turning all by itself.

Marie grabbed Henri's hand as the hiss of the spinning wheel grew louder still: *SHHHOOOM. SHHHOOOM. SHHHOOOM.*

The whole house was shaking, but the children didn't care. They kept hugging Grand'-mère and crying until she gently pushed them away.

When Grand'-mère turned to look reprovingly at Henri and Marie, the roar of the spinning wheel grew so loud the children clamped their hands over their ears. *SHHHOOOM. SHHHOOOM. SHHHOOOM.*

Below them, the front door crashed open. "Papa, Mama! What's happening?" It was Josephine's voice shouting over the hissing of the spinning wheel. She and her new husband had been awakened by the sound and come running to the rescue.

A moment later, Josephine appeared at the top of the ladder, followed immediately by her husband.

Grand'-mère nodded in satisfaction at the sight of her eldest grandchild. When she spoke, her ghostly voice cut right through the hissing reverberation of the spinning wheel. "Good. You are all here. Listen closely, my kinfolk. I said I wanted you to buy fifty Masses for the repose of my soul. I told you every single day. But not one Mass has been said."

SHHHOOOM. SHHHOOOM. SHHHOOOM. The roar of the spinning wheel made dust fall from the rafters. Dishes shattered in the kitchen below.

The children glared reproachfully at their parents. They had all assumed Henri had done his duty by their grand'-mère.

Josephine exchanged glances with her husband. She stepped forward. "We will pay for the Masses, Grand'-mère," she shouted above the roar of the spinning wheel.

Grand'-mère's dark eyes bore into her son's face. "Your daughter knows right from wrong," she said. "Do you?"

Henri flushed with shame and stared at the floor. He had not done right by his mother and he knew it. What kind of an example was he setting for his children? He glanced at his wife, who nodded.

"We will pay for the fifty Masses," Marie shouted over the roar of the spinning wheel. "We promise, Grand'-mère."

"We promise, *Maman*," Henri echoed. "Fifty Masses for the repose of your soul."

Grand'-mère leaned back, satisfied. The spinning wheel abruptly stopped its supernatural whirl.

THE SPINNING WHEEL

The sudden silence came as a shock. Henri rubbed his tingling ears. Trust *Maman* to make a huge fuss when she didn't get her own way. He'd always said she had a will of iron. Grand'-mère beckoned to her eldest granddaughter. "Come kiss your grand'-mère goodbye," she said. Unafraid, Josephine hurried toward the glowing figure and hugged Grand'-mère Duchene tightly. She whispered: "Can we not buy you one Mass at least, Grand'-mère?" Her young husband nodded vigorous agreement from his spot by the ladder.

"One Mass, *cherie*," Grand'-mère said, patting her back gently. "But your father still owes me fifty!"

Josephine laughed tearfully. "Agreed!"

A moment later Josephine was hugging empty air over a dark and silent spinning wheel. Grand'-mère was gone. The little ones wailed a bit, but they were not as disconsolate as they previously had been. They knew Grand'-mère wasn't gone for good. She'd always be close by, watching over them.

Henri pushed hastily passed his son-in-law and hurried down the ladder.

"*Mon cher*, where are you going?" Marie called as he put on his coat and hastened to the front door.

"I am going to the church to buy fifty Masses," Henri called back. "If I don't, who knows what else *Maman* will do!"

Pocketing his wallet, Henri raced out into the dark night to awaken the bewildered priest and make good on his promise.

Resources

Asfar, Daniel, and Edrick Thay. *Ghost Stories of America*. Edmonton, AB: Ghost House Books, 2001.

Asfar, Dan. *Ghost Stories of Michigan*. Edmonton, AB: Ghost House Publishing, 2002.

Barber, Sally. *Myths and Mysteries of Michigan*. Guilford, CT: Globe Pequot Press, 2012.

Bishop, Hugh E. *Haunted Lake Superior*. Duluth, MN: Lake Superior Port Cities, Inc., 2003.

Botkin, B. A., ed. *A Treasury of American Folklore*. New York: Crown, 1944.

———. *A Treasury of Railroad Folklore*. New York: Crown, 1953.

Boyers, Dwight. *Ghost Ships of the Great Lakes*. Cleveland, OH: Freshwater Press, Inc., 1968.

Brunvand, Jan Harold. *The Choking Doberman and Other Urban Legends*. New York: W. W. Norton, 1984.

———. *The Vanishing Hitchhiker*. New York: W. W. Norton, 1981.

Coffin, Tristram P., and Hennig Cohen, eds. *Folklore from the Working Folk of America*. New York: Doubleday, 1973.

———. *Folklore in America*. New York: Doubleday & AMP, 1966.

Cohen, Daniel, and Susan Cohen. *Hauntings & Horrors*. New York: Dutton Children's Books, 2002.

Crane, Mary Beth. *Haunted U.S. Battlefields: Ghosts, Hauntings, and Eerie Events from America's Fields of Honor.* Guilford, CT: Globe Pequot Press, 2008.

Dewhurst, C. Kurt, and Yvonne R. Lockwood, eds. *Michigan Folklife Reader.* East Lansing: Michigan State University Press, 1988.

Donaldson, Karen Hoisington. *Haunted Houses of Michigan.* Self-published, 1988.

Donohoe, Kitty, and Pasqua Cekola Warstler. *Bunyan and Banjoes: Michigan Songs & Stories.* St. Johns, MI: Kidfolk Press, 1987.

Dorson, R. M. *America in Legend.* New York: Pantheon Books, 1973.

Eberle, Gary. *Haunted Houses of Grand Rapids.* Grand Rapids, MI: Silver Fox Publishing, 1994.

Editors of Life. *The Life Treasury of American Folklore.* New York: Time Inc., 1961.

Erdoes, Richard, and Alfonso Ortiz. *American Indian Myths and Legends.* New York: Pantheon Books, 1984.

Fasquelle, Ethel Rowan. *When Michigan Was Young.* AuTrain, MI: Avery Color Studios, 1981.

Flanagan, J. T., and A. P. Hudson. *The American Folk Reader.* New York: A. S. Barnes & Co., 1958.

Franklin, Dixie. *Haunts of the Upper Great Lakes.* Holt, MI: Thunder Bay Press, 1997.

Godfrey, Linda S. *Weird Michigan.* New York: Sterling Publishing Co., Inc., 2006.

Hammond, Amberrose. *Ghosts and Legends of Michigan's West Coast.* Charleston, SC: Haunted America, 2009.

Hauck, Dennis William. *Haunted Places: The National Directory.* New York: Penguin Books, 1994.

Hivert-Carthew, Annick. *Ghostly Lights.* Chelsea, MI: Wilderness Adventure Books, 1998.

Holub, Joan. *The Haunted States of America.* New York: Aladdin Paperbacks, 2001.

Hunter, Gerald S. *Haunted Michigan.* Chicago: Lake Claremont Press, 2000.

———. *More Haunted Michigan.* Chicago: Lake Claremont Press, 2003.

Kuclo, Marion. *Michigan Haunts and Hauntings.* Lansing, MI: Thunder Bay Press, 1992.

Leach, M. *The Rainbow Book of American Folk Tales and Legends.* New York: The World Publishing Co., 1958.

Leeming, David, and Jake Page. *Myths, Legends, & Folktales of America.* New York: Oxford University Press, 1999.

Lewis, Chad, and Terry Fisk. *The Michigan Road Guide to Haunted Locations.* Eau Claire, WI: Unexplained Research Publishing Company, 2013.

Lyons, Sandy Arno. *Michigan's Most Haunted: A Ghostly Guide to the Great Lakes State.* Troy, MI: SkateRight Publishing, 2007.

Oleszewski, Wes. *Ghost Ships, Gales, & Forgotten Tales: True Adventures on the Great Lakes.* Gwinn, MI: Avery Color Studios, 1995.

———. *True Tales of Ghosts & Gales.* Gwinn, MI: Avery Color Studios, 2003.

Otto, Simon. *Walk in Peace: Legends and Stories of the Michigan Indians.* Grand Rapids: Michigan Indian Press, 1990.

Pattskyn, Helen. *Ghosthunting Michigan*. Covington, KY: Clerisy Press, 2012.

Peck, Catherine, ed. *A Treasury of North American Folk Tales*. New York: W. W. Norton, 1998.

Pitkin, David J. *Ghosts of the Northeast*. New York: Aurora Publications, 2002.

Polley, J., ed. *American Folklore and Legend*. New York: Reader's Digest Association, 1978.

Reevy, Tony. *Ghost Train!* Lynchburg, VA: TLC Publishing, 1998.

Robinett, Kristy. *Ghosts of Southeast Michigan*. Atglen, PA: Schiffer Publishing Ltd., 2010.

Schwartz, Alvin. *Scary Stories to Tell in the Dark*. New York: Harper Collins, 1981.

Scott, Beth, and Michael Norman. *Haunted Heartland*. New York: Warner Books, Inc., 1985.

Skinner, Charles M. American Myths and Legends, Vol. 1 & 2. Philadelphia: J. B. Lippincott, 1903.

———. *Myths and Legends of Our Own Land*, Vol. 2. Philadelphia: J. B. Lippincott, 1896.

Spence, Lewis. *North American Indians: Myths and Legends Series*. London: Bracken Books, 1985.

Stonehouse, Frederick. *Haunted Lakes*. Duluth, MN: Lake Superior Port Cities, Inc., 1997.

———. *Haunted Lakes II*. Duluth, MN: Lake Superior Port Cities, Inc., 2000.

Untermeyer, Louis. *The Wonderful Adventures of Paul Bunyan*. New York: The Heritage Illustrated Bookshelf, 1945.

Zeitlin, Steven J., Amy J. Kotkin, and Holly Cutting Baker. *A Celebration of American Family Folklore.* New York: Pantheon Books, 1982.

About the Author

S. E. Schlosser has been telling stories since she was a child, when games of "let's pretend" quickly built themselves into full-length tales acted out with friends. A graduate of Houghton College, the Institute of Children's Literature, and Rutgers University, she created and maintains the award-winning Web site Americanfolklore.net, where she shares a wealth of stories from all fifty states, some dating back to the origins of America. Sandy spends much of her time answering questions from visitors to the site. Many of her favorite e-mails come from other folklorists who delight in practicing the old tradition of who can tell the tallest tale.

Also in the Spooky Series by S. E. Schlosser: